THE
LONG WAY
HOME

DAN HEALY, BOB FROMHARTZ

The information contained within this book is strictly for educational and entertainment purposes. We do not condone the actions displayed in this book. If you wish to apply ideas contained herein, you are taking full responsibility for your actions.

The Long Way Home. Copyright © 2021 by Dan Healy and Robert (Bob) Fromhartz. All rights reserved. Printed in the United States of America. No part of this book may be used or reproduced in any manner whatsoever without written permission except in the case of brief quotations embodied in critical articles and reviews. For information, please email Dan Healy at Healydanny@att.net.

First Edition, Second Printing

Cover design by Charlote Licayan
("Relic 88" on 99designs.com)

Photographs by Sarah Jones Decker, Emma Hileman, Jon Taylor, Amelia Cary, and myself.

Editing and text design and layout by Colten Poe

ISBN 978-1-7365236-0-5

Dedication

This book is dedicated to my wife Carmen. Her sacrifices and determination kept me strong and her love and support carried me to my final steps. She was with me for every mile and never gave up on me or my dream.

Table of Contents

Glossary of Thru Hiking Terms ii

Foreword iv

1. Springer Mountain Georgia 1
2. North Carolina 9
3. Tennessee 22
4. Southern Virginia 31
5. Maine 35
6. New Hampshire 58
7. Vermont 78
8. Massachusetts 91
9. Connecticut 99
10. New York 105
11. New Jersey 114
12. Pennsylvania 119
13. Maryland & West Virginia 137
14. Northern Virginia 142
15. Fort Lauderdale & Central Virginia 164

Acknowledgements 189

Glossary of Thru Hiking Terms

AT: Appalachian Trail

Blazes: Trail direction markings

Bubble: An expanded "Tramily" of hikers.

Cowboy Camping: Under the stars, in front of the fire.

False Summit: A peak is reached, and you find the actual summit is higher up and further away.

Flip Flop Hike: Starting at one end and for some reason, going to the original destination and hiking back to where you stopped.

Hiker midnight: 8:00 pm or dark.

Leap Frog: Passing other hikers and them passing you.

NOBO's and SOBO's: North or South bound hikers.

Nero Day: Nearly a Zero... A short day on the trail.

PUD's: Pointless ups and downs.

Purple lines on the maps: Trail towns that I stopped at.

Safety Meeting: After a hard day on the trail, Smoke or sip and unwind with whatever relaxes you.

Section and Day hikers: People that drive to and park at roads crossing trails and hike for a day, or do a multiday section hike.

Slack Packing: Using shuttles or other transportation options to pick you up or deliver you to trail heads, so you can use a lighter day pack for a day.

Stealth Camping: Making camp in the woods.

Trail Angels: People that help hikers without asking and ask for nothing in return. They give advice, food, drinks, directions, rides and more.

Trail Magic: Usually roadside generosity by strangers.

Trail Names: Given to thru hikers by family or other thru hikers. My trail name was "TAR" (Trees and Rocks).

Tramily: The people you meet, hike with and see at shelters and campsites. They become part of your "trail Family"

WFS: Work for Stay in N.H. Huts. Exchange room and meals for work.

Yogi-ing: Begging food, water, rides, etc. from strangers.

Zero Day: Resting, chores, and resupply w/ zero miles.

Foreword

Before you read Dan Healy's story, you should know a little bit more about him. His family and I picked him up in March 2019 at Damascus, Virginia where he took his final step. I talked to an older resident and told him why I was in Damascus and about Dan's hike. He shook his head and said, "Why"? He said he couldn't understand why anyone, never mind a 73-year-old man would want to walk that far.

Dan and his wife Carmen and I have hiked hundreds of miles in the North Carolina mountains and when we'd stop at road crossings, people would stop and ask us a variety of questions about our hike. We'd politely answer that, "we eat food" or "no, we didn't see any bears", or "we'll try for fourteen miles today". The hardest question to answer is, "Why?". People say they climb Mt. Everest because, "it's there". With Dan, I think there were many reasons why.

As we hiked the mountain trails over the years, we all grew to appreciate the scenery, the solitude, and beauty of nature itself. That's when Dan's dream began. As time went on the dream began to be an obsession that would take years of planning, saving, and convincing friends and family (especially Carmen, his wife). Years before the planned start date, Dan began working a second job and saving his money to pay expenses that are needed to make the hike possible.

Backpackers are strange animals... They become so obsessed by their hobby/sport or, as some say, disease or sickness. They become aware of every ounce they carry and will weigh every item and every meal. Then they will plan for resupply either in a trail town, or through mail drops sent from home. We've seen hikers carrying packs loaded with sixty pounds that didn't seem to enjoy the hike, or at least the uphills.

Dan met his wife Carmen in Fort Lauderdale and while they were dating, he talked about hiking and how he thought she would love the woods. He convinced her to take a multi-day hike in the North Carolina mountains. As the start date neared, Dan bought an engagement ring and he planned to propose on the top of a 5,300 foot peak on the first night.

It was Carmen's first hike and she wanted to bring some of her essentials. I suggested to Dan that he should reduce the weight of her pack, so she gave some essentials to Dan to carry. He turned to me and asked if I'd carry the heavy engagement ring to lighten his load. I made an exception and agreed to carry the ring. We started up a very long uphill that would take us to the top. Dan probably had forty-five or fifty pounds in his own pack, including some essentials that Carmen wanted. He didn't want to overload her on her proposal day, so she had maybe twenty-five pounds in her pack. I struggled with the uphill climb as I always do and was glad Carmen was with us as she struggled more than me. They were both behind me and I started taking more frequent breaks and rest stops. This went on for hours until I heard footsteps coming up behind me. I looked back and here comes Dan with Carmen's pack tied to his own pack. I gasped for air as he went by me with Carmen following. I yelled something to him about me carrying his heavy stuff (the ring) but he kept going out of sight.

We finally made the top where I unloaded the heavy ring. We found some wildflowers and Dan got on one knee and completed the mission. I went from ring bearer to photographer. By the way... She said, "Yes".

Carmen joined our hiking group and became very good at it. Dan carried eighty pounds or so up that mountain. Love makes a man do strange things.

There is more a reader should know about Dan before reading about his thru hike. Like me, Dan was born in Connecticut and in the 1940's and 50's, learned a New England work ethic. His family moved to Fort Lauderdale in the late 50's (like mine) and that's where he grew up and still lives. He was very close to his mother and his sisters, all who remained close in Florida. He worked two jobs for a long time supporting his first wife and two sons. A few years ago, he lost his youngest son to cancer, then, more recently his sister also was lost to the disease.

Dan became the rock of the family and at that time was beginning to get serious about completing the AT thru hike. He started raising money to find a cure for cancer, and before he was finished, he was credited with over $7,500 in donations to the American Cancer Society.

Each day in a thru hike on the Appalachian Trail has a dose of adversity in it. You'll see how a very determined hiker handles each stumbling block as they occur. Most adversity is a result of things like the weather and conditions on the trail itself. Then there's the adversity and losses we all face in life. Life goes on for family and friends and there are a lot of ups and downs needing our attention and sometimes our physical presence. Things can happen when you are thousands of miles away in the woods for months.

Fortunately, for all the adversity there is the opposite. The birds calling, the deer grazing, and most importantly the people met, and the friends made along the way. These people become a temporary family and often turn into lifetime friends. I know sections of the hike have seen violence and other problems, but Dan and I hiked a lot of trails together and never had a problem. You meet some characters, but they are mostly in the woods for the same reason you are. To enjoy the scenery, smell the clean air, get some exercise, and learn more about their surroundings.

When Dan was ready to start his Appalachian Trail thru hike on Springer Mountain in Georgia, I'd talk to others about his upcoming effort. When I mentioned his age, they might roll their eyes and ask how far I thought he'd go. I always told them the same thing. Out of the thousands leaving Springer in March and April heading north and the hundreds leaving Mt. Katahdin in Maine heading south, If I had to bet on someone finishing, all my money would be on Dan. That doesn't mean it was going to be easy or guaranteed, but I knew how focused and determined he was to succeed.

Some Appalachian Trail statistics:

In 2017 about 3,735 thru hikers left Springer Mountain, heading north and 489 left Mt. Katahdin in Maine heading south. From 2011 to 2015 the completion rate was between 25% to 27%. In 2016 that rate fell to 20%. Keep in mind these numbers are put in by the hikers so they are only as good as a hiker's honesty. 2017 completion numbers were not in yet. I saw one hiker's cost of his hike numbers, and they were $11,708 total or $66 per day or $5.35 per mile. One doesn't have to spend a lot of money. Years ago, on our first hike, Dan and I met a young (about eighteen-year-old) thru hiker who had the trail name "Minnie", as in Minnesota. He stayed in campsites and shelters every night because he couldn't afford hotels or even hostels. A resupply meant a detour into town, buy some groceries, and return to the trail to sleep. That means no Uber, no Lyft, no shuttles, and no public transportation. On Dan's last night on the trail, he met an eighteen-year-old that had averaged almost sixteen miles a day for a month, with no zero days. That's pretty speedy, but did he smell the roses?

I guess if there's a message in this, it would be, save your pennies until you can do the hike with a little comfort. Running out of money can end a dream in a hurry.

–Bob Fromhartz

Chapter One

Springer Mountain Georgia

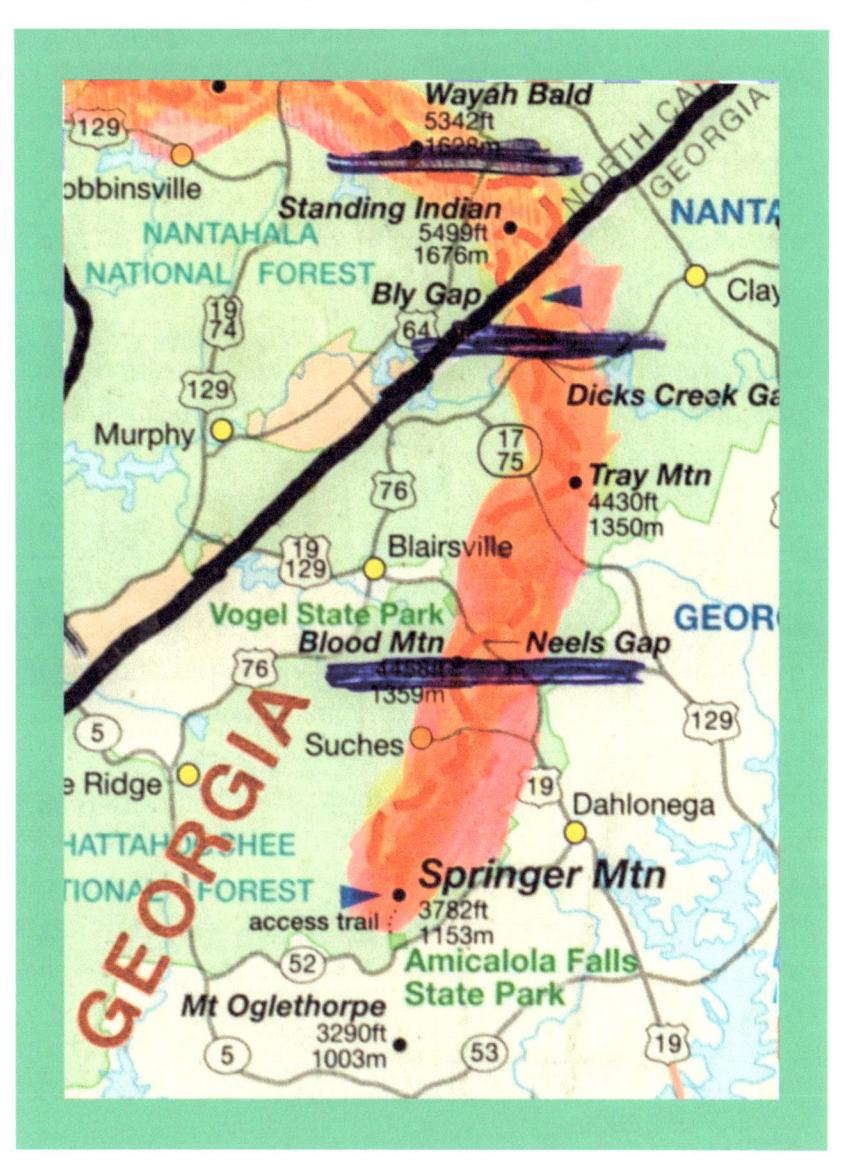

I planned on starting on April 15, 2018, but the weather forecast wasn't good, so I delayed my start a week. I chose to skip the approach trail from Amicalola since I was in good shape and had already checked and rechecked my gear on previous hikes.

My wife Carmen and I are huge NASCAR fans, and we knew of a very famous driver, Bill Elliot, who lived in nearby Dawsonville Georgia. We decided to spend the night there and I'd begin my "walk" the next morning. Carmen and I had hiked from Springer a few years before, and we knew there was a Forest Service road that crossed the trail nine tenths of a mile North of the starting point. The road was not well maintained so, Carmen and I rocked and rolled for about forty-five minutes until we reached the Appalachian Trail.

There were two other vehicles in this procession that followed us to say their goodbyes and give me a "proper" sendoff. Carmen, her best friend Altagracia, and our son in law Nery. Two more vehicles held my hiking buddy Bob and his dog "Maggie May", my sister Anne Marie and her husband Larry. We first had to celebrate conquering the forest service road, then there were some emotional goodbyes.

Bob and Maggie walked with me back to the starting point on Springer Mountains summit. The walk was cold, but easy as Maggie raced ahead appearing and disappearing ahead of us. Bob took some pictures of the plaques on the top, and one of Maggie looking at me as if to say, "are you crazy or what?"

I then began my long hike to Mt. Katahdin, that turned into a long adventure across fourteen states. In less than a mile Maggie and Bob reached his truck at the road. We said our "see you later's," as we'd be seeing each other a lot in the next few weeks. Bob and Maggie were on their way to his house in the mountains of North Carolina, and they would help me with resupply. That was the plan. But, as I found out in the months ahead, plans can change in a hurry.

Due to the late start, I was unable to reach my goal of the Gooch Mountain Shelter. The shelter was at mile 15.8, and 3.6 miles before it I had to set up camp at road crossing near Cooper Gap. I was almost out of water and there was none to be found nearby so I tried to figure out how I'd ration what was left. A large group of Boy Scouts came and began preparing a site to set up their tents. I considered "yogi-ing" (begging from strangers) to see if they had extra water, but before I could get up, one of the adult leaders came over and introduced himself. Like most people you meet on the trail, he had a long list of questions. I always try to be respectful and tactful while trying to keep the conversations to a minimum so I'd be able to make it to Maine someday. We talked for a few minutes and as he walked away, he asked if there was anything, I needed… bingo. He not only gave me water for dinner and breakfast, but he made a donation to my "Cure for cancer" campaign through the "Crowd Rise" website. I tried to call Carmen but my phone said "No Service" and I was already missing her and my family. Whenever I could call them, I'd get a huge emotional lift.

The next day I hoped to make the summit of Blood Mountain, and stay in a shelter, but again I came up short. I ended up "stealth camping" near a dirt road at Woody Gap. Stealth camping is another thru hiking term meaning to set up camp on a flat spot in the woods. I ended up with company when a woman and her son joined me and found another flat spot. Later, another thru hiker joined us. He was from Montana, and had two big cameras hanging from his neck. He said he was trying to take one picture every hour while he was on the trail. He was a big guy, and he said he had to lose some weight. I told him I could see a weight loss in his future. It's well known on the AT that the trail will get you in shape if you keep putting one foot after the other.

I was up early but the Montana hiker was long gone. I was convinced I needed to take advantage of shelters, as I refuse to give up my hot breakfast. A lot of hikers get up, stuff their pack, eat a Pop Tart or an energy bar, wash it down with some water, and they're gone. Shelters mean less packing and easier meal preparation, but the downside is the mice and the chorus of "snorers".

The next day started out nice but quickly turned into a cold rain as I reached the peak of Blood Mountain. Before I made the decision to actually do this hike instead of just dream of doing it, I took dozens of multiday backpacking hikes and I got along with the animals (two and four legged) and the mountains, but I did have some fears. I worried about hypothermia because I'm thin and have no fat to insulate my body. I descended Blood Mountain in a wind driven downpour that, at times, fell sideways. I was about to experience some "trail magic", that couldn't have come at a better time. Trail Angels perform their "magic" by the goodness of their heart and without expecting anything in return. They show up unannounced at road crossings with food, drinks, and words of encouragement. They also show up at times hikers need help and give rides or directions to make the journey a little easier.

The storm was still raging when I arrived at a road crossing with a small parking lot and a restroom. While I waited for the storm to pass, it just got worse. I heard a guy in a nearby car yell "Do you need help?". I said, "No, I'm okay". Ten minutes later he asked again and I accepted a ride into town where I found lodging for the night.

I thanked the Angel and thousands of miles north I would see him again. It's a small world. Now I had to see how to get back on the trail the next morning. There are many options and some were not available ten years ago. I would end up using them all. Uber, Lyft, shuttles, public transportation, walking, or sticking out your thumb. The lodge I found had a shuttle, so that was settled. The weather didn't improve that night, so I took a zero day.

The old song said, "I never promised you a rose garden." I never expected this adventure to be easy, but day five turned out to be just plain ugly. No rain early on but fog and cold hung over the first few miles. I passed through a place called Mountain Crossing at Walasi-yi where the trail passes through the center of a building that has been there since the 1920's. It now houses an outfitter and a hiker hostel that is known for helping struggling and new hikers. They have hikers empty their packs and go over and weigh every item, making recommendations as to what goes and what stays. I decided to skip this exercise and headed to the north exit door.

My mind is constantly doing the math of time and distance. I know I'll have to stick to my plan as closely as possible if I'm going to make it to the finish line in Maine. I also had to consider that Baxter State Park would close in mid-October and Mt Katahdin would close with it. I started slowly and have already taken more zeros than I should have. I have to make those days and miles up somehow.

The weather improved, and I was able to pick up the pace and I started making it to the shelters which allowed me to get earlier starts in the mornings. With all the rain, everything stays wet. It's not easy to crawl out of a warm sleeping bag and put on cold wet clothes that you wore the day before. Nothing dries in the woods unless you have sunlight and there isn't much to find on the trail. During this stretch I was the benefactor of the most elaborate "Trail Magic" I'd see on the entire hike. It was a tough day of P.U.D.s (a hiker term for Pointless Ups and Downs). These are some of the gap-to-gap hikes without much to see.

It was raining and cold as I descended to a road crossing that had a small parking lot, where I saw some vehicles and tent like structures, and found tables filled with food and hot and cold drinks, energy bars, donuts, muffins, and much more. All this was done by a local church and their members. They were even giving out free, knitted wool ski caps, knitted by church members. I had some hot tea and a muffin and thanked the Angels for their unexpected and much appreciated generosity. That afternoon I hiked into the Tray Mountain Shelter. I hadn't been dry since I started, and it was getting old. I was hoping to make Plum Orchard Shelter that night and the North Carolina state line the next day.

That was the plan, but it wasn't meant to be. I made it to a road crossing at US-76 in Dicks Creek Gap. A Trail Angel was parked in his van and saw me shivering. He suggested I walk a half mile up the highway to the Top of Georgia hiker hostel. He said it was a great place to dry out and he was right. I was glad I took his advice.

I knew that once I was in North Carolina my friend Bob would be able to help me with resupply and more. As it turned out, I needed a lot of his help. His home in the mountains was close to the trail and to the Great Smokey Mountain National Park where I'd be hiking for a week or so. I had about 130 miles from the state line to the 6,600 foot Clingmans Dome. It would be the highest elevation I'd see on the entire hike. It was also where I'd lose Bob's help as he'd be heading to Florida soon.

Chapter Two

North Carolina

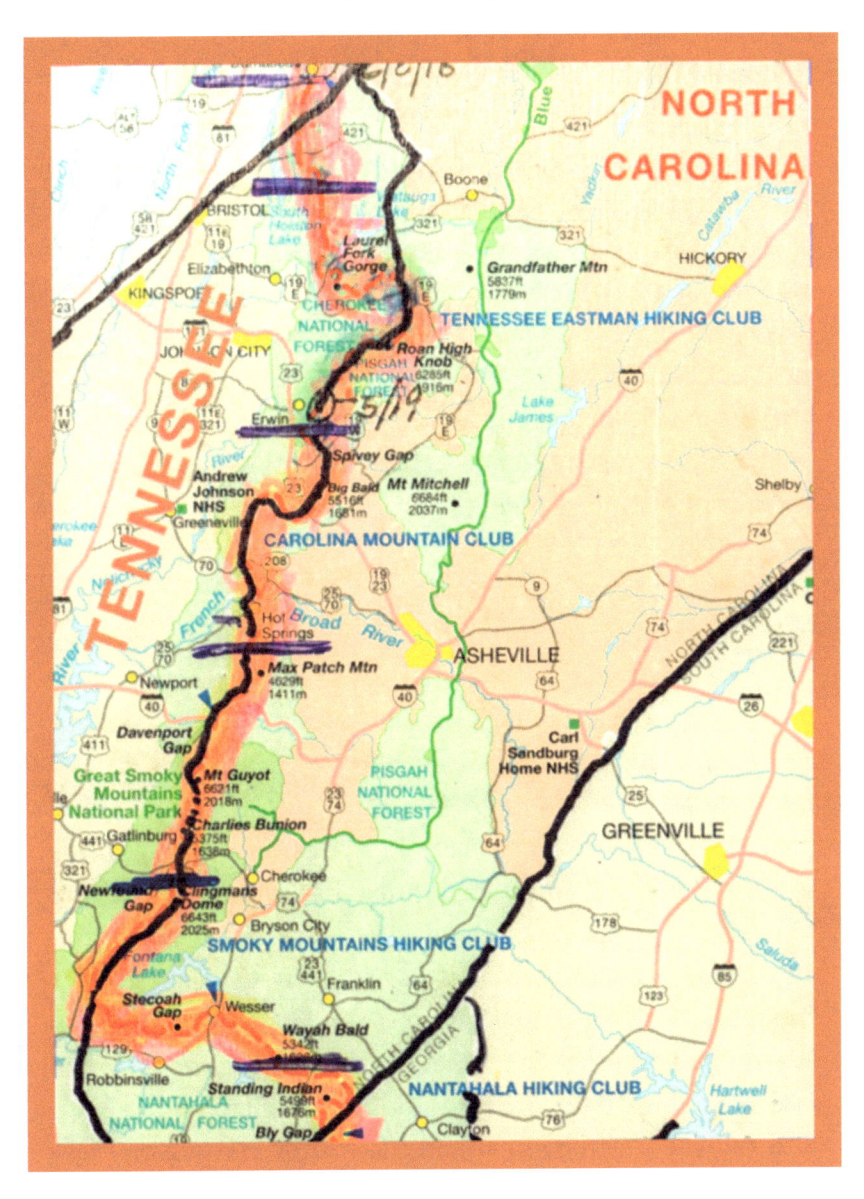

I'm not sure how the AT shelters were named but some were interesting if not entertaining. My first night in North Carolina would be at the Muskrat Creek shelter. In the last few days, I'd caught up with some of the friends I'd made in Georgia. Nobos are what they call North Bound hikers and if you end up in a loose group of hikers (called a bubble) that although they don't always hike together, they stay close and pass or be passed by others in the bubble. At times you stay in the same shelter or in the same trail towns. Others stay together closer and for a longer time and they call them "tramilies" as in "trail family". Everyone has different speeds and habits and even casual hikes will have hikers drifting miles apart and arriving at campsites or shelters at different times. Many hikers would rather hike alone and enjoy the nature and solitude and others want to "blah, blah" their way to the next stop.

When I got to the Muskrat Creek shelter it was almost full. The shelters usually hold six to eight hikers. I always try to arrive at a shelter by late afternoon. This gives me time to relax, take care of some chores and gives me a better chance at finding room at the shelter.

My first meeting with Bob came unexpectedly on my first full day in North Carolina at a place called Deep Gap. This was the same place my wife Carmen, her son Angel, Bob and I hiked into a few years earlier. We were hiking North and were headed to Carmen's car parked at Deep Gap. The last five or six miles were through some very heavy, and cold rain. We were all freezing and when we saw the car, we all broke into a run to strip down dry off, put on dry clothes, and jump into the car which by now had the heater blasting on high.

Angel was a teenager at the time and a little self-conscious, but he couldn't get out of his wet clothes fast enough. This time my grand entrance into Deep Gap went differently. Five miles from my destination, I started feeling tightness in my left upper leg. It went quickly from uncomfortable to painful. I was moving so slow that I began to worry if I could make it at all. The uphills were just slow but the downhills were very painful.

The trail itself had turned very rocky where footing became an even bigger issue. I saw a hiker headed toward me and realized it was Bob and Maggie. Bob had waited for me knowing I was going to be there that afternoon. He brought some soda, beer, sandwiches, and snacks and was feeding a large group of hikers while waiting for me. Some of the hikers told him they passed me and I was having problems. Bob decided to walk up the trail and meet me. He took my pack and we both made it down to the dirt road and parking area. The good news is he saved me some food and a beer for my reward. Some trail heads are on rough and tumble dirt and/or gravel roads. Deep Gap is on one of these and you reach it off of North Carolina sixty-four about twenty miles west of Franklin North Carolina.

Bob had visited a massage therapist in Sylva North Carolina that helped his always ailing back. She also used acupuncture and I knew I wouldn't be hiking for a few days but I wanted to be recovered enough to get back on the trail. After three treatments I could see some improvement so, I tried slack packing for a five mile section, then ten miles the next day. Bob was helping by dropping me off in the morning and picking me up in the afternoon. As the leg felt better my pack decided to start falling apart at the seams. I would stuff something in it and whatever went in, something else would squeeze out a torn seam somewhere. It was eight years old and had a lifetime guarantee. I didn't expect much but we made calls to the company and they sent me a new pack by next day air. To get the credit we had to cut up the old one and send them a few pictures of it. I was pleasantly surprised to say the least.

I began a fifteen mile day, and the plan was to meet Bob at a road we picked out on a map. It turned out the road was closed and we couldn't make a connection. Bob had to drive twenty miles to come in from another direction and we finally found each other. The next day I did fourteen miles and met Bob at the NOC (Nantahala Outdoor Center).

The river is known for its' whitewater rafting. It's also the place that twenty-three years earlier Bob and I took a rubber ducky two-man raft down the Nantahala. **We hit a huge rock and both of us exited the raft in different directions. I had my paddle and found a boulder to hang on to while Bob tumbled underwater for a long time before he figured out which way was up and he grabbed some air. We somehow finished the raft trip with one paddle. After that experience Bob said "No more whitewater" and we decided to try backpacking.**

There was a long six mile descent down to the Nantahala River and the next day I faced a six mile climb to Cheoah Bald. Carmen and I had also hiked this section a few years earlier and I knew what to expect. Having previous experience didn't make it any easier. Bob dropped me off early and I started the climb. The visibility was bad as a fog hung over the mountain.

By the time I finished the six mile climb and reached the Cheoah Bald peak the fog had burned off. The Bald offered a stunning view of one range of mountains after another. I could see a deep valley ahead and my destination of Stecoah Gap. While finishing this day I reconnected with the hiker from Montana that I met on my second night in Georgia. It's common on the trail that hikers have and use trail names. If someone doesn't have one It becomes another hiker's job to make one up. For the rest of the hike he was to become "Big Sky". The name fit him perfectly.

    I crossed the road and saw Bob's truck with a group of hikers standing and sitting. Bob had a cooler full of beer, soda, water, snacks and sandwiches. There was a big party going on. The party ended and I made it to a shelter for the night. The following day I made it to the Fontana Dam Shelter. It's one of the stops where hikers sometime spend a few days and resupply or pickup mail at nearby Fontana Village. The Shelter is also known as the "Fontana Hilton". It had a good crowd spending the night and I stopped to talk with other hikers when Bob and Maggie showed up. There is a road and parking area very close to the shelter. It's also, close to the dam that I would cross the next morning. For now, we went back to Bob's for one of my last nights in his cabin.

    The next morning, we were back at Fontana picking up the trail where I left off. The thirty-five mile section to Clingmans Dome is considered one of the most difficult of the AT. The White Mountains of New Hampshire are considered more difficult. The shelters in this stretch usually have full shelters plus tents, tarps, and hammocks spread out all over. It makes for some great stories around the campfire, but you'll also get to enjoy a "snorer's serenade". Then there will be some people talking all night and the aroma of unwashed clothes and people wafting in the night air.

I felt great after a good dinner and a good night's sleep at Bob's place. As I started across the dam, I turned to wave. This would be a special day as my destination was a shelter called "Spence Field".

Spence Field Shelter, Photograph taken by Emma Hileman.

Bob and I were both working for Sears back in 1965 I was nineteen and Bob was twenty-one. My father while coaching me about life would tell me to work for a large stable company that treats their employees fairly and has good benefits. He also said work hard, be on time, and stick with it. Bob and I had a lot in common and would have a beer

after work sometimes. We usually called them meetings, so someone may hear Bob tell me there was a "meeting" at 5:30 and your attendance is required.

Around 1990 Bob and his wife bought five acres on the side of a mountain at about 3,000 ft. elevation. We started going up for a week almost every year just to get a little relief from Florida's heat and humidity. After our whitewater rafting disaster on the Nantahala River, we swore off water sports and decided to take up hiking. We did a few day hikes where we'd run into backpackers and talk to them about their equipment and travels. Then we started doing some overnight hikes. We then began to plan a thirty-five mile hike from Clingmans Dome to Fontana Dam. Bob wanted to start at the top (6,600 ft.) thinking it would be easy and mostly downhill. I'm a runner and Bob was a couch potato, but we were determined to finish it. We planned on taking two nights and three days to complete the hike. There was a shelter at mile nine or ten and we made it by one 1:00 pm. I didn't want to stop that early, so I talked Bob into doing six more miles to Spence Field.

By this time Bob was about out of downhills and he started hugging trees. We had the wrong food (ham sandwiches and peanut butter) and didn't bring enough water. About a mile out from Spence, I went ahead, and Bob dragged in about an hour later. Bob, who never walked more than a mile or two, finished his first sixteen-mile day. Before Bob arrived, I went 100 yards or so to a water source. I started pumping through a filter when I heard some rustling in the woods. I looked up and saw a large black bear staring at me. He was between me and the shelter, so I had to walk around him and keep my eye on him until I made it to the path to the shelter. After Bob dragged in, the bear came up to the chain link fence that was closed around the shelter and started looking for food. I have to add, the Park Service decided a couple years later to remove all the fences around the shelter.

They said if you want to feed the bears, go for it.... The problem apparently was caused by hikers feeling so safe behind the fence they would feed the bear for entertainment. When the fences went down, they stopped feeding them in a hurry. Whenever a bear causes property damage around a shelter, the shelter will usually be closed until rangers are reasonably sure the bear is no longer in the area. If a bear injures a person, the authorities must hunt it down and euthanize it. It's a shame because we are in the bears' home. Black bears are vegetarians and will only bother confronting a human if they are cornered or protecting their young. Usually one has to worry more about the two-legged animals.

Well day one was pretty ugly and day two was going to be worse. We decided to save a mile or two by taking Eagle Creek down to Lake Fontana. It looked okay on the map, but looking back now, we probably should have followed our original plan. We made it down the creek with the trail crossing the creek fifteen times. It started easily jumping on rocks and as we lost altitude the water kept getting deeper (and colder) until we were up to our waists holding our packs up. We found out wet feet will blister fast. When we reached the shore of the lake, we saw a boat pulled onto the shore. No one was there and we weren't lost but we *couldn't find the trail. We could see the trail on the map that led back to Fontana Dam where my van was parked. That's when the owner of the boat and another fisherman came up and said "hello". We explained where we came from and showed them the map. They said they thought they knew where the trail was, and we all went looking. We followed several trails that went nowhere until we all gave up. Bob, looking tired and with his feet bleeding asked (begged) for a boat ride over to the dam where my van sat.*

They finally agreed and we soon finished our first real backpacking hike. Bob swore he'd never do something that crazy again. His feet were a mess and swollen and he was completely worn out. He kept saying "never again", but as we were driving back to Fort Lauderdale, we both started to plan our next hike. That's how it started and led me to this point where I'm climbing the same mountain that we came down all those years ago. We learned a lot on that hike about what to bring and what not to bring as far as food, equipment, and clothing. Both of us began buying good basic equipment like tents, sleeping bags, cooking kits, first aid kits etc. We've done enough backpacking in the last twenty years to wear out some very good gear.

That's enough ancient history, so let's get back to 2018. On the way to Spence Field, the trail passes Shuckstack mountain. There is a fire tower at the top with great views of the Smokies. I made Spence Field by late afternoon and by dark the shelter was almost full. The next day was a big one. About seventeen miles with some rough terrain and a climb up the 6,600 feet of Clingmans Dome. The AT actually follows the North Carolina and Tennessee state line through the

National Park. You can step in Tennessee with your left foot and then in North Carolina with your right foot. The plan was to meet Bob in the Clingmans Dome parking lot around 4:00 pm, but the weather wasn't cooperating today and as I passed the 5,000 foot level the rain started to turn to hail and sleet. When I finally made it to the parking lot, a worried Bob was waiting. His truck was running with the heater going and we headed back to his cabin for the last time. He would drop me off tomorrow where he just picked me up.

Now I was truly on my own. I was now headed to one of my favorite trail towns. Hot Springs, North Carolina is one of the few towns where the white blazes that mark the trail go right down Main street through the center of the town. There are places to eat, drink, and stay or if you're just passing through there is a good outfitter on the main street. It was still about seventy-five miles ahead of me, so Hot Springs was the incentive for the next five days or so. The first night out I stayed in the Icewater Springs shelter. The shelter was packed, and the overflow slept in tents and hammocks.

Everyone was polite and respected "Hiker midnight" (8:00 pm). On the second day I stopped at a rock formation called "Charlies Bunion" where at 5,500 feet I had an awesome view of a valley below. Full shelters would be the norm for the next month or so.

The next day's hiking brought me some pleasant memories. Around lunch I passed a shelter called "Tri Corner Knob", where fifteen years earlier I took my beautiful Hispanic wife to be up this mountain to propose to her. *I asked Bob to carry the ring as I didn't want Carmen to find it in my pack. Bob complained the whole time about having to carry the "heavy" ring up a mountain. Carmen was on her first hike and she was struggling so I tied her pack onto mine to make the hike easier for her. When we finally reached the peak, I picked some wildflowers and after getting the ring from Bob, I got on one knee and proposed. Thank God she accepted. Bob went from "heavy ring hauler" to "cameraman" and took a picture that today hangs on our bed's headboard.*

Tri Corner Knob Shelter, Photograph taken by Sarah Jones Decker

My next short-term goal was Max Patch. The trail goes directly over the top and has some 360-degree views. It's accessible by car so there are usually day hikers and sightseers moving around the trails and the top. I arrived there around noon and while I was enjoying the scenery and activity, some of the other thru hikers in my "Bubble" joined me. Later that evening we migrated to the west side of the slope and enjoyed one of the best sunsets I've ever seen. Hot Springs was only twenty miles away so I decided to camp somewhere before the town.

    I made it to the Laughing Heart Hostel. Hostels usually have three options to choose from. Tenting ($5-$15), Bunk House ($20 to $30), or private room ($25 to $30). I decided to treat myself to the "quiet" of a private room. I had a mail drop with my supply of food and personal items waiting at the post office. Carmen was an absolute Godsend. Before I started my trek, I spent months preparing a list of trail towns and estimated times of arrival. Carmen gathered the supplies, packaged them and sent them in a timely manner. Unfortunately, rural post offices keep different and ever-changing hours and are always closed on Sunday. This accounted for too many "Zero" days.

    The next trail town would be Erwin, Tennessee. I left Hot Springs, crossing the bridge over the French Broad River. The trail follows the riverbank for about a mile. There were other thru hikers camped along the river and I heard one yell "Hey TAR". It was my friend from Montana, Big Sky. My sister gave me my trail name before I left. Like many people she couldn't understand why I wanted to do the hike. She said all I'd see for months would be "Trees and Rocks". So far, she was right. Big Sky and I caught up on trail news and I began my climb up the steep rocky face of Rich Mountain. A rock outcrop on the way, called "Lovers Leap" offered views of the French Broad River below. I chugged along over the next five days of seemingly endless and pointless ups and downs (PUD's). As I neared Erwin, my reward appeared at the final summit when I was treated to a great view of the Nolichuky River about 1,000 feet below.

Crossing Fontana Dam in North Carolina...
Thirty-five miles to Clingmans Dome

Chapter Three

Tennessee

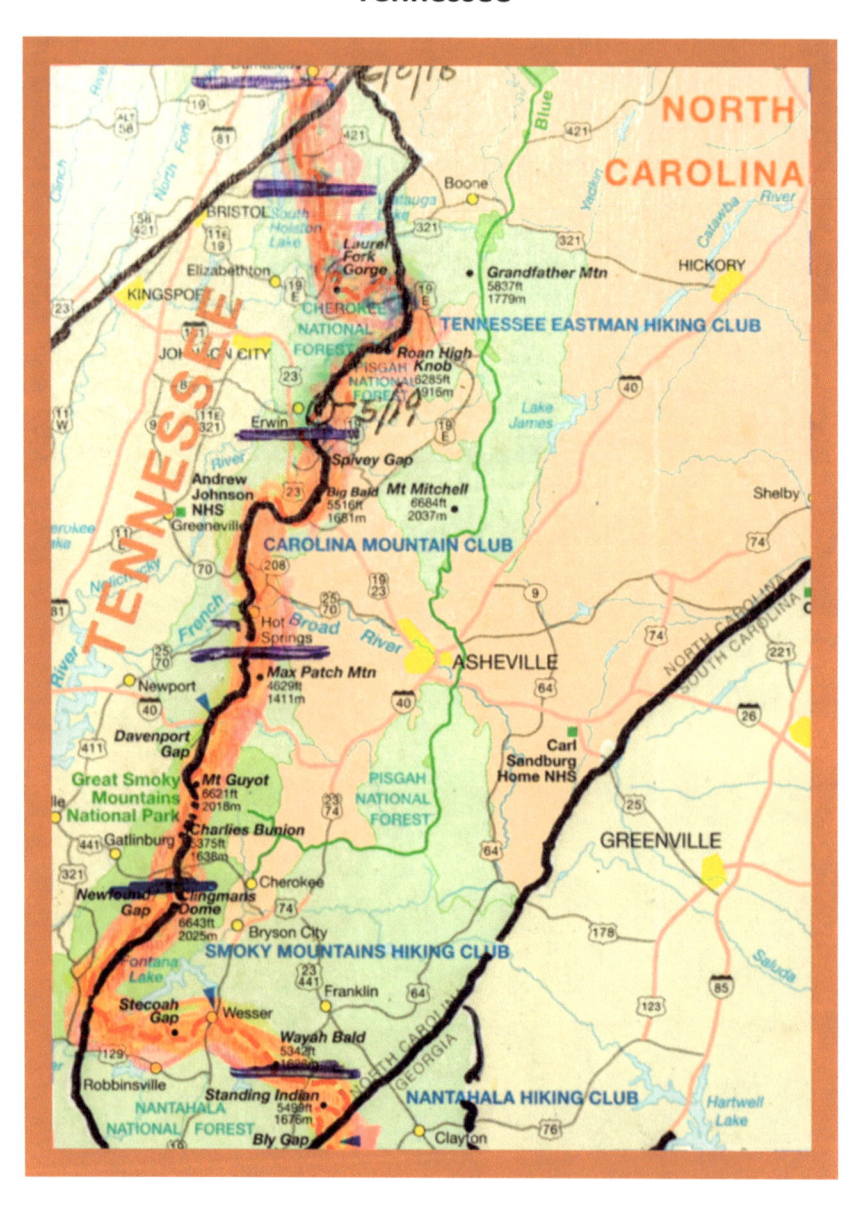

"Big climb today out of Erwin", I thought to myself. The town is at 1,600 foot elevation and I was heading to the summit of Mt. Unaka, about thirteen miles away. About two miles from the 5,200 ft. peak, I passed a place called "Beauty Spot Gap". It was like a mini "Max Patch" back in North Carolina. There was a small parking lot and at the top I met a middle-aged couple that had walked to the summit for the views. They approached me and asked some of the questions thru hiker's answer on their trek. I shared some of my experiences with them and added a plug for my "Cure for Cancer" cause. I left them and on the other side of the parking lot I found a beautiful campsite.

While checking the site out I found the water source was a piped spring. I always filter my water, but spring water gives you added confidence the water won't be contaminated. It was getting late in the day, so I decided not to push on to the shelter and camp here. As I set up my tent another hiker joined me and we began chatting. He was from New Zealand and had taken time off from his job to do a section of the AT. In the weeks and months ahead, I'd meet many "section hikers". Some take ten, fifteen, or even twenty years or more to complete the hike. They are usually unwilling or unable to complete a thru hike which has to be done within one year. The New Zealand hiker and I hit it off and shared some dinner and trail stories before retiring. Apparently, dinner didn't agree with me and in the middle of a very dark night I had to make my way to a wooded area for some relief. There were no other symptoms and by morning I had a small breakfast and hit the trail.

As I checked the elevation profile on my map, I could see it was the kind of day I liked. The biggest ascent first thing, then the rest of the day ridge running with little elevation change. I caught up with some of the other hikers in my "bubble" and we hiked together for the rest of the day. At 4:00 pm, another hiker mentioned a hostel about .6 miles downhill to the east. I decided to make my way to the hostel while the others decided to push on to the shelter.

The owner of the "Greasy Creek Friendly" hostel was Connie, and she greeted me warmly at the door. She asked that I remove my boots and then said I needed to wash my hands. This seemed reasonable and I complied. The bunkhouse was in the barn behind the main house and Connie asked me to keep the door closed, as mice were a problem. Staying in shelters gets one used to living with mice and chipmunks. These pests are common and relatively harmless in the Southern Appalachians. Most shelters have pulley contraptions to hang your food to keep out mice and bears. If you camp in the woods, you can hang your food from a rope in a tree. You don't want to sleep with the food for obvious reasons.

Connie made a run to town and came back with hamburgers for dinner. I couldn't finish my dinner like I usually do after hiking all day. I went to bed, but around 10:00 pm I woke to the same issue I had the night before. I put on my headlamp and made my way to the main house and the bathroom. I made a half dozen trips, back and forth until I collapsed in a chair in the living room. I thought about making my way to an emergency room but decided to wait. By this time, it was morning and Connie came out and knew I had problems. She suggested I spend another night or two until my stomach settled down. She let me move to the front porch to eliminate the midnight travels from the barn.

There were a couple guys doing work-for-stay on the property. One was attending a local college and was studying herbology. He said he would make me a tea from plants growing on the property that were known to settle stomachs. He said it would restore my digestive system, so I agreed to try it. The results were nothing short of amazing and on the fourth day I packed up and left for a ten mile hike to the Roan Mountain shelter. At 6,200 ft. it is the highest shelter on the AT and I had penciled it in as a "must stay". I guess I was still weak as the last two miles were a struggle. When I reached the shelter, it was almost full and the only space left was on the second level. The shelter was a unique, cabin-like design with windows in the gable end and a vertical ladder to the second level. I had to make a choice between the second level and setting my tent up outside the shelter. It was already getting cold and it looked like it would be in the thirties overnight, so I dragged my pack up the ladder. As it turned out, I had the second level to myself with the added space and privacy.

Roan High Knob Shelter,
photograph taken by Sarah Jones Decker

I didn't set an alarm and when I awoke, the shelter was empty. I must have needed the extra sleep. It was foggy when I started and the descent was tricky, with the trail covered in large, slippery rocks. The weather continued to deteriorate, and I was soon slogging through a heavy downpour. The trail began filling with water that cascaded down the mountain. I ended up on my butt a few times and my pace went from slow to a crawl. I guessed my speed at one mph at this point, and I passed a trail junction that said, "Overmountain Shelter .5

miles". I had only managed eight miles at this time so I decided to have lunch at the shelter. I had read about this shelter and remembered it was a barn that had been converted into a shelter. I came around a bend in the trail and the barn/shelter came into view. There were already three hikers in the shelter, so I decided to call it a day and spend the night. Hikers kept trickling in and before I knew it, the shelter was full and the overflow folks were setting up tents and hammocks in and around the shelter. Whenever there is a large crowd, there will be some that want to party and talk all night. I finally got to sleep at 11:00 pm or 11:30 pm and had a dream about putting on clean, dry clothes in the morning.

Back on the trail early, I now had 385 miles under my belt. It was a beautiful, clear morning for a walk in the woods. It was somewhere in this section I had a strange encounter with the local bovines. I came to a pasture with a stile that had to be climbed to get in (these are fairly common where the trail crosses private lands). I somehow lost the trail but saw an opening in some barbed wire that would get me through to the other side. As I tried to maneuver under the barbed wire, my pack got hung up on the wire. After struggling for a while, I decided to get out of the pack. I was then able to get myself out and after a few more minutes, I got the pack loose from the wire. At that point I had one leg in the pasture and the other leg back on the trail. I looked up and to my surprise there were nine or ten cows in a semi-circle, staring at me. I apologized for interrupting them and continued on my way.

After a short ascent to the summit of Hump Mountain, then a long descent to Elk Park and crossing the North Carolina-Tennessee state line again. I had another of

Carmen's much anticipated mail drops hopefully waiting at the Elk Park Post Office. Since it was a Saturday, I would have to take another "Zero" and pick up the resupply on Monday.

The hostel at 19E was great. A new bunkroom with mattresses, a bar serving local craft beer and the owner/host was also the bartender. This was a special treat because Carmen and I have been home brewing for about five years now.

I stayed in the woods with my new supply of food to keep me going. In thirty more miles I was In Hampton Tennessee. Staying in another hostel called "Boots Off". When I arrived, they said they had no rooms, but I could "stay in in the bus". I must have looked like a deer in headlights. The owner tossed me a key and said, "check it out". The bus was in a corner of the property and when I opened it, I was surprised. It had been converted to a one room rental with a shortened queen bed. I took it and he gave me information on shuttles leaving for town. After a town visit that included the Dollar Store, a Subway, and quick stop for some beer, I made the return trip of the shuttle. I felt great compared to a few weeks earlier when my stomach was giving me problems, and I looked forward to the next fifty miles crossing into Virginia and making it to Damascus, another friendly trail town. Damascus has a big "Trail Days" festival every year in mid-May. Hikers, young and old, flock to this event every May for seminars, music, and comradery. Many are hikers from previous thru hikes looking to meet up with their trail friends from years before. I was focused and running behind, so I kept pushing to reach Damascus, but I didn't plan to stay.

Huge "thank you" to the trail maintainers

I still had miles to go, so the next morning I was out early. The first stretch was a short road walk down to Lake Watauga. The trail had been relocated due to some earlier flooding and I had to follow signs that led me back to the trail. The detour took me almost all the way around the lake, then across the top of a dam. After more road walking, I finally located the trail and stopped to call Bob as I saw a cell tower and figured this may be my opportunity. We had a good talk and I told him where I was. He said my "SPOT GPS locator" showed I had not left the "Boots Off" hostel yet. Bob and Carmen had used my SPOT signals to track my entire hike and depending on the signal availability knew where I was at any given moment. My heart sank as I turned to look at my shoulder where SPOT was supposed to be but wasn't. It then occurred to me that when I was at the Boots Off Bus the previous day, I put it on the hood of the bus so Carmen and Bob would get a stronger signal. In the rush thru the rain that evening and the hurry to get back to the trail the next morning, I left for the trail without it and never thought about it. I told Bob where I left it and he said he'd make some calls and try to track down the tracker (no pun intended). I called Bob later in the day and he said they found it and they said a thru hiker was planning a thirty mile hike the following day. They gave Bob his name, and he said he could catch me and would deliver the SPOT. The hiker's trail name was "Five Mile", but Bob and I think it should be changed to "Thirty Mile". Five Mile caught me at a shelter and we both spent the night swapping stories.

Chapter Four

Southern Virginia

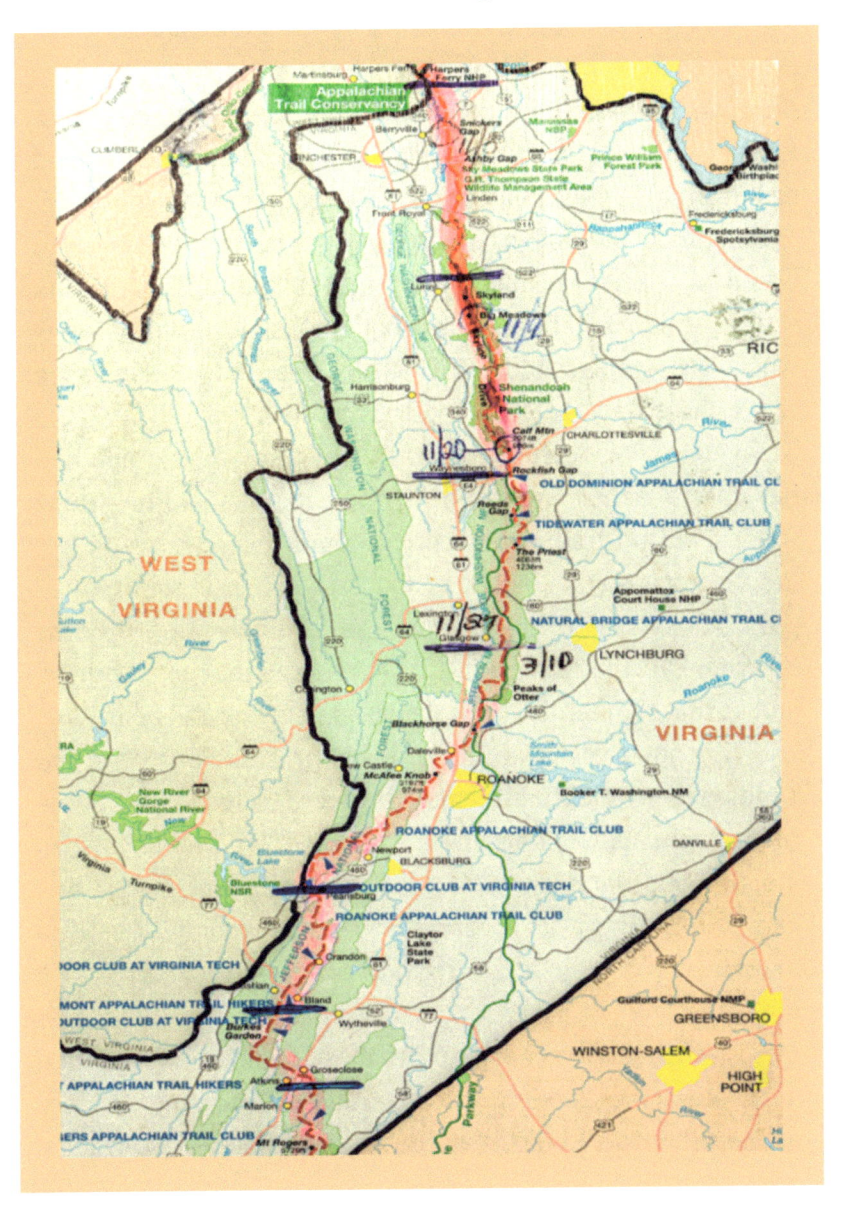

Newly armed with my SPOT and the GoPro camera, I felt a renewed sense of energy. Virginia, with its 520 miles of AT is by far the longest state I'd hike through. It's state number four and it leaves ten more to go. I'm still planning to make Mt. Katahdin in mid- October but I know I need to pick up the pace and increase my speed and decrease my zero days. Entering Virginia and then Damascus, I had great weather and easy terrain. Soon I was on a main road through the town. Then onto an old railway called the Virginia Creeper Trail, that was now used for biking and hiking. I talked to a tourist and she asked some standard questions, so I asked her if she knew where a hostel was located. She said she thought she saw a sign a short way back, so I headed to find it.

At the Woodchuck Hostel, I met the owner, Paul, and decided to treat myself to a private cabin instead of a bunk room. Paul offered kitchen privileges to his guests and like most hostels sold a variety of snacks and frozen foods. I had pizza and a pint of ice cream. The latter became my trail favorite. Paul made breakfast for the guests the next morning, and at that moment, my whole world began to fall apart.

I'm not sure if it was a phone call or a text, but I received a message from Carmen that I needed to call my sister, Anne Marie, right away. Anne Marie is a year and a half older than me, and another sister, Susie, is five years younger than me. Earlier in 2018, my younger sister Patty passed away at fifty-nine years old, from a rare form of cancer. Two years before that I lost my youngest son, Aaron, to liver cancer at thirty-nine. In the last fifty years, our family had endured more than its' share of losses. I also lost a brother to a boating accident and another to sudden infant death syndrome. My mother is the rock of the family, as she cared for my father for years before he passed away from multiple sclerosis in 2000. When I reached Anne Marie, I could tell from her voice that something was wrong. She said our mother was in the hospital and it didn't look good. Anne Marie said I might want to think about coming home, but she said she already asked Mom if she wanted me to come home and she said "No, I know how much this hike means to him." I told her I was on my way and I'd call her with the details.

I didn't know where to start. I told Paul what happened, and he said there was a regional airport about forty miles away. I then called Carmen and she began searching for flights. After hours on the computer and the phone, she booked a flight and Paul found a shuttle driver available to get me to the airport.

When I walked into Mom's hospital room, I got a big smile from her. I spent the next three weeks taking turns with my sisters, doing a bedside vigil. Her health continued to deteriorate as her frail ninety-three-year-old body was ravaged. I recalled that in past years I had wondered how I could ever go on without her when this day came. She had truly been my soul and inspiration. But that day had reluctantly arrived. I was in no mood to go backpacking, but I had promised my mom I would go back and finish what I started.

I knew my plans had to change as I'd lost another three weeks in Fort Lauderdale and combined with a late start in April and too many zero days. It was now too late to continue North bound as Mt Katahdin closes in mid-October due to the weather. My only option was to fly to Maine, hike to the northern terminus of the trail, and begin heading south. This is a fairly common tactic called a "flip flop" thru hike. On June 28th, I boarded a flight to Bangor, Maine.

I had been to Mt. Katahdin twelve years before, when I was in Maine competing in a track event at the University of Maine in Orono. On a whim I decided to drive to Baxter State Park and see the 5,300 foot peak for myself. The mountain stands out as there are no other mountains nearby. That day I turned back because the trail was strenuous. There would be no turning back this time as I had to reach the summit before heading back to Damascus.

Chapter Five

Maine

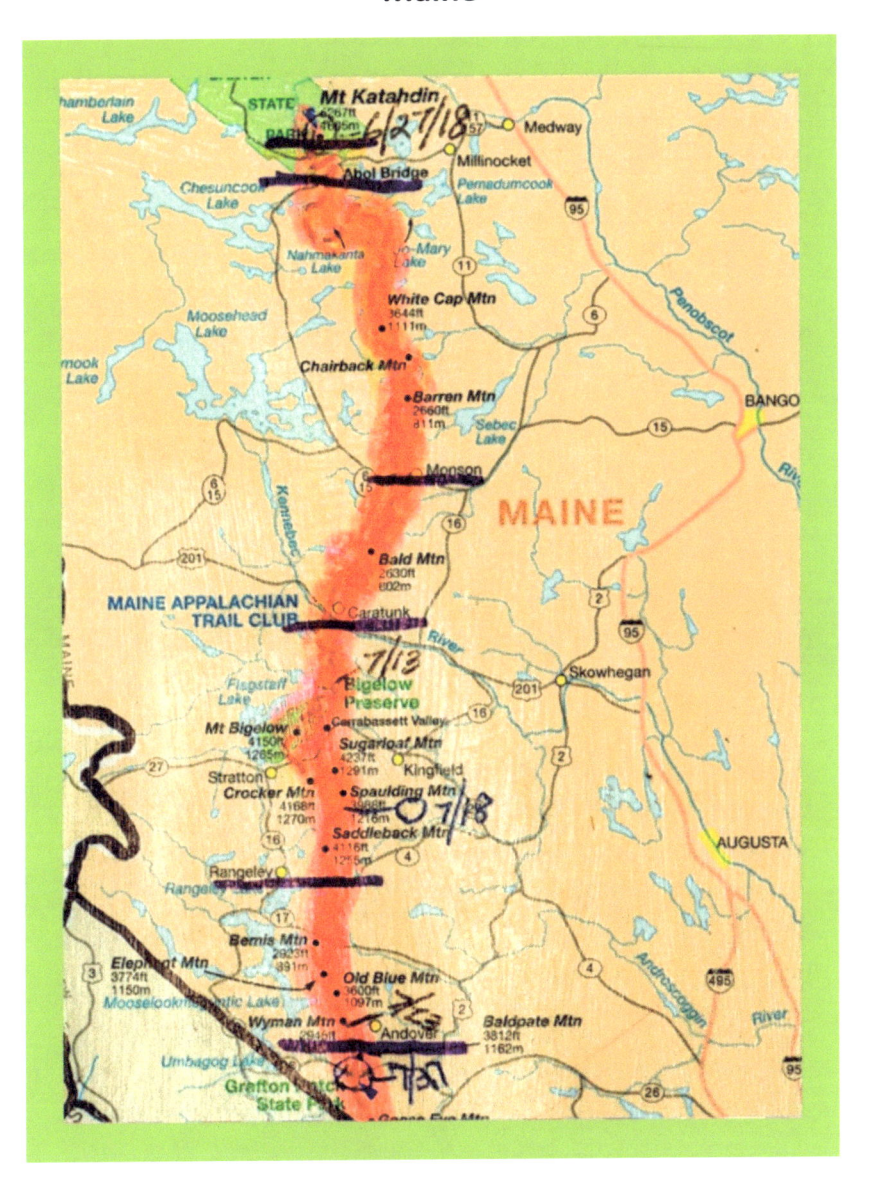

I touched down in Bangor and walked to the bus station about a mile away. The bus brought me to the town of Millinocket about seventy miles from Bangor. This town is as close as any to the state park, but still twelve miles away. While sitting in the bus station, I saw a couple come in wearing back packs. I was about to make an enduring friendship that I cherish to this day. Even though I was probably fifty years older it didn't seem to matter as we hit it off immediately. They were both in the Marines and I was in the Air Force in a previous life. While we were enjoying our stay in a hostel, the manager gave us a quick description of what we could expect to find in Maine. Porcupines, leaches, rock climbing, and best of all, how to resupply for our trek through the "Hundred-Mile Wilderness." This section is well known to thru hikers and takes extra planning and care to complete.

My new friends and I would summit Katahdin in the morning, then descend to a hostel for the night. This would be my first official day as a "South-bounder". That night at the hostel I met another hiker with his very large pet pit bull. He talked about some of the other dogs he had over the years and as he described them, they all sounded aggressive to me. I asked if there was a reason he liked aggressive dogs and he said, "because I want them to be able to kill someone if they have to". I made a quick judgement that he may be a little too intense for my liking, so I made it to my room for the night. Later in my hike I found I was too quick to judge him.

Baxter Peak, the summit of Mt. Katahdin is on the right

    Our trip to Baxter State Park slowed as we approached the entry gate. After a long line of traffic, we made it in and headed to the Ranger Office to register for the climb. They had loaner day packs and insisted we use them. That gave us all an idea of what difficulties we were about to face. It's about a five mile climb and the forest quickly turns into steep rocks. It was so extreme, steel rebars had been drilled into the rock at different points so we'd have foot and hand holds through the worst sections. At one point I looked up at a pointed ridge going skyward. No trail just rocks with 2,000 to 3,000 ft. drops on both sides. I remembered thinking to myself "I may be able to climb it, but I'll never be able to get back down." It turned out the descent wasn't that bad as there were other options like sliding on one's butt, or backing down, or choosing another route. At the summit is the iconic "A frame" sign. On that day there were a dozen hikers at the sign, waiting to have their picture taken. I had thought about what pose I'd like to have of me at the summit. When my turn came, I climbed on the top of the "A" and gave my best Usain Bolt impression with my arms pointed skyward. What a rush. The exultation defies description but was similar to the first time I completed a marathon.

No time to linger, as all I could think of now was that I had 1,700 miles or so to Damascus and an end to my "walk". I made my way down safely, taking every precaution. It was scary and slow but I knew any misstep would probably stop me for a period too long to make up. Katahdin attracts large crowds other than thru hikers. One person can reserve a shelter that easily can accommodate eight to ten people. There are about six shelters and you go from one to the next one and ask if you can stay with them. I was accepted by a nice couple from Utah on my first try. As we all crawled into our sleeping bags, the wife asked if anyone would object to her saying a prayer. That was the only time on my hike that this happened and I was glad she did it. There were no objections. As for myself, I prayed every morning and as the hike continued the prayer expanded and became even more personal. I always finished by kissing a picture of my mother and sister before hitting the trail.

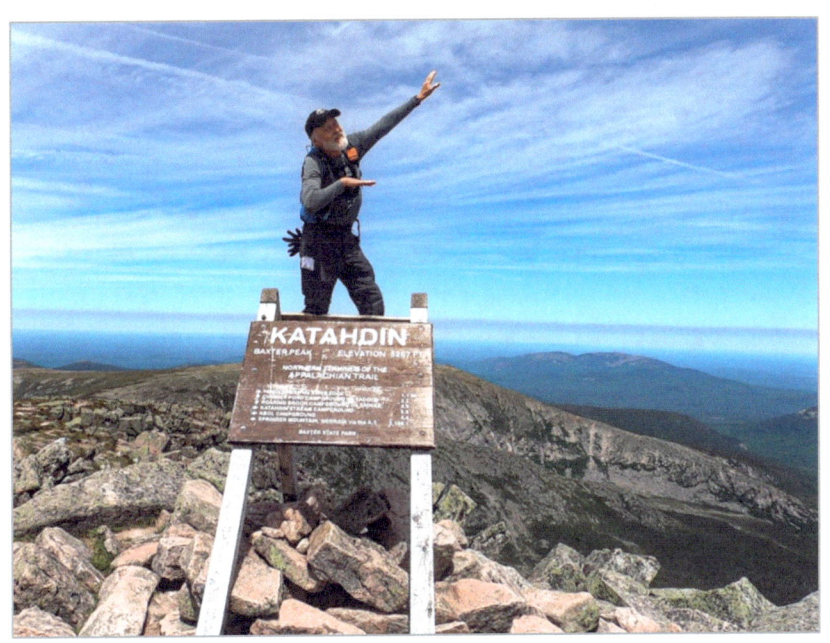

"TAR" on the A frame

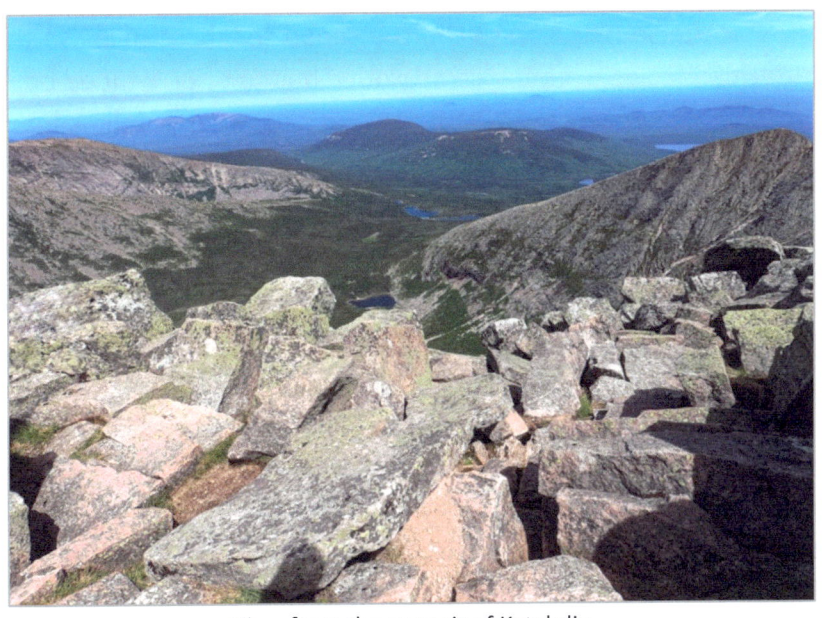

View from the summit of Katahdin

39

As usual I was the last hiker out the next morning. My plan was to hike out of Baxter State Park, about ten miles. Then to a shelter three miles past the park. Like many plans, things can and do go wrong. By mid-afternoon the sky darkened and the rains came. I gambled it would be a little shower, but it was still coming down when I reached the ten mile mark. There was a campground and small restaurant with a group of hikers gathered outside the door trying to keep dry. Among them I saw my new friends that I met at the bus station and summited Katahdin with. Ryan and Lauren had already indulged themselves with a big juicy hamburger. I was soaking wet and shivered from the cold. The group of hikers were ready to finish the last three miles to the shelter (they are called a "Lean-to" in Maine). I was thinking about joining them, but the thought of some hot food and a dry place to eat it won out over that idea in about thirty seconds.

After eating I wasn't in the mood for more miles so I decided to see what the campground had to offer. I ended up paying five dollars for a campsite and another five dollars for an all you can eat breakfast. When planning this hike, I tried to think of any negative situations I'd be faced with. One I worried about was setting up my tent in the rain. The rain started again before I could get dry from the last downpour. I had a rainfly for my tent and another one for my pack. I also had waterproof stuff-sacks to keep my clothes and gear dry. I also had a lightweight, microfiber towel to dry everything off, if and when, the rain ever stops. I guess I was more worried about the rain and cold because I'm so thin, the combination of cold and wet could lead to hypothermia.

I left the campground and passed a sign that welcomed me to "The Hundred Mile Wilderness". It's really only eighty-five miles but I guess it wouldn't have sounded as formidable if they said, "Eighty-Five Mile Wilderness". After three miles I found Ryan and Lauren still in the shelter. They were trying to dry their clothes and gear so we hung out for a short time and they stayed with me for the rest of the Wilderness. This will be the longest we will go without going through or near a trail town. You have to carry eight to eleven days' worth of food, but a few years back when the AT Lodge in Millinocket found an accessible spot near the trail about halfway through. For a fee they will cache your resupply and give you some "secret" directions to find your order near the trail. That means you can carry 10 pounds of food instead of Twenty. Ryan, Lauren and I all paid the required fee.

Our first night we camped next to a huge lake with beautiful views. We all jumped in for a swim. I'm already seeing why they say Maine is the most difficult and the most beautiful of the fourteen states that I would pass on the hike.

The next day we got a good taste of why, even what looks like an easy day in Maine, can turn out very slow. Looking at a topo map there would be very short climbs and mostly downhills. Yet the trail was a mess of gnarly, tangled roots, rocks, and mud. It seemed like we needed three steps sideways for every step forward. We didn't expect an escalator, but one would've been nice. We made it to the Wadleigh Shelter where a large stream ran near the shelter. We all had to cross the stream on a log that had fallen across the water. One of the hikers in our group ventured downstream a short way and found an eddy that was perfect for a quick dip. We all took turns going downstream until the last two to go came running back and said they were chased by a very irate beaver. I never saw a beaver or a moose in any of the fourteen states.

The next day was warm and sunny and we were looking forward to finding our resupply cache in the woods. The directions were a little vague but after wandering around awhile we saw the dayglow ribbons tied on branches for us to follow. About 100 yards in off the trail we found the cache under a big blue tarp. Our resupplies were in white five-gallon plastic buckets with our names on the labels.

While in camp that night we discussed the challenges that laid ahead. It included White Cap Mountain at 3,700 feet and the Chairbacks which are a series of five peaks between

2,200 and 2,600 feet. Though not very tall, they would prove to be very intense; with vertical slabs of granite that were often so smooth and slippery, we were forced to the outside edges where we could find something we could hold. Lauren and Ryan outpaced me with their youth and by the time I reached the summit, I found them waiting. We found out later the temperatures were over ninety that day as Maine had a rare heat wave. I was exhausted and dehydrated and immediately dropped my pack and took off my shirt to wring it out. I felt lightheaded and laid down spread eagle on a granite slab. The rock was cooler than the air and a light breeze came thru. It was just the break I needed. We all recovered quickly and packed up for the downhill ahead.

No sooner had we reached the tree line when the most amazing thing happened; Trail Magic. On a mountaintop in the Hundred Mile Wilderness, two young women, one of them just off a successful Northbound thru hike a few days earlier and with a friend accessed a forest road and carried backpacks loaded with tasty goodies like candy bars, cookies, chips, donuts, soda, fruit, and Gatorade. Trail magic and trail angels are usually found at road crossings but these beautiful ladies were far from the nearest roads. We said our thank you's and good bye's and started a long gradual descent to our very first river crossing at the west branch of the Pleasant River.

When we arrived, I was surprised at how wide it was but, luckily for us, it was also very shallow. Most of the crossing was only ankle deep but the river bottom was covered with round, slippery rocks. We all made it through this time, but there were many more crossings in our future, and we were not always as lucky. There was a Ranger and an Appalachian Trail Conference Volunteer sitting in camp chairs when we completed the crossing. We had a good conversation and they gave us some good advice about what lied ahead. The lean-to where we spent the night was just short of the summit and about twenty-six miles to the end of the "Wilderness". But we first had to conquer the other "Chairbacks" one by one. They were not even named, but each had a signpost with a number at the peaks.

The next day, I was involved in a serious altercation with a tree, and the tree won. Since our south-bound hike began the three of us hiked at about the same pace. They were faster on the uphill and I was usually faster on the descent. On this day we had long stretches of relatively flat terrain. But, like the last few days, the trail was full of rocks, roots, and mud. These conditions require hikers to look down to see every foot fall. I was behind Lauren and Ryan and had to look up every now and then trying to keep them in sight. We were moving at a good pace and I didn't notice when they ducked under a tree that had fallen across the trail. I plowed into the tree with my forehead and staggered back a few steps seeing stars. Everything seemed okay, but that night I had a pinching-like pain in my neck that was so bad I couldn't sleep at all. I even tried sleeping sitting up, but still no relief.

The next morning, I made it back to the trail to find every time I looked down, I'd get the same pain only much worse. I was very tired and my mind began to wander. I thought I may have some serious damage and have to stop my hike, or worse, need surgery. But then reality would return to me and I thought "I'm in the Hundred Mile Wilderness, and there is no 'plan B' in sight. I'm going to have to suck it up and walk my butt out of here." I hoped for a better night's sleep that night, but it never came. The next morning, I was awake but totally exhausted. I thought I may have passed out and caught some sleep during the night, so I hit the trail again. The trail improved from the day before and my pain was down, so I decided to take an optimistic approach. I thought maybe I just had a pinched nerve in my neck, and I needed a little time to recover. The optimism seemed to work and I hoped for some sleep that night.

It worked. I slept so well I wanted to stay in the sleeping bag longer that morning. Knowing Monson and an end to the "wilderness" was only half a day away got me up and going. When I hit the trail, I realized the pain was gone and I felt whole again. Now I could concentrate on a new problem. I hadn't seen my wallet in days. It contained Carmen's picture, my driver's license, and three credit cards. In all my planning for this hike, I had not planned for this. I guess I'd have to figure it out at my stop in Monson.

We made it to the road crossing to Monson, and there was already a group of hikers waiting for a shuttle to town. We shared high fives and congrats as this section is one of the highlights of the hike. There were several choices of hostels in Monson and from what I heard on the trail, Shaw's was supposed to be a solid choice. Lauren and Ryan went to "The Lakeshore House", another good choice. I was still thinking about my lost wallet and the time I'd probably have to spend replacing what it contained.

I mentioned before that it's a tradition among thru hikers to give each other trail names. These names have been used for years and I've been told it had something to do with safety. You're hiking every day and sleeping every night with strangers you don't really know. It's probably wise not to give others personal information, so everyone uses a trail name. Some name themselves, some (like me) are named by their family, and others start the hike without a name but are soon given one from fellow hikers. I was honored to name three hikers this way. After days of hiking with the Montana mountain man, he became "Big Sky". I also named Lauren "Thumper", because of her plodding style of heavy step hiking. I named Ryan "Fixit" because my pack was a critter victim one night in a shelter and ended up missing the buckle to my hip belt. I was trying to find a solution the next morning when Ryan came over and rigged me up a temporary fix that worked.

    Our shuttle driver was super cool and shared some trivia on our way to town. As we drove into the driveway, he offered us a soda or a beer. That was the easiest decision I had to make all day. As I opened it a hiker walked up and asked, "Are you Dan Healy?" Puzzled, I replied "Yes, but where do I know you from?" He confidently exclaimed, "You don't, but I recognized you from the picture on your driver's license." He then handed me my wallet. I was so relieved and elated, I gave him a big bear hug. He had found the wallet in a lean-to in the "Wilderness". There's a saying among thru hikers that states, "The trail will provide". This wouldn't be the last time the trail had provided for me.

    I went inside Shaw's to register and decided after nine and a half days in the "Wilderness", that I deserved a private room and a zero day to recover. I was looking forward to their homecooked breakfast with their trademark blueberry pancakes. I slept like a baby, dreaming about the pancakes. My zero day was a busy one. I took a shuttle to another town that had an outfitter. Boots are usually good for 400 or 500 miles and mine had 600 miles so I replaced them while I had the chance. Then I went to the ATC (Appalachian Trail Conference) to register my hike. I had tried to do it before I started but had trouble with the website and gave up.

 I met up with Fixit and Thumper and we had lunch by a lake. Back at Shaw's later that afternoon, I was chilling in the main house living room when a guy walked in that I immediately recognized as the trail angel that had helped me find a hostel in Georgia when I was on the verge of hypothermia. This "small world" coincidence blew me away. He was just in town for some business which made the meeting even more odd.

 I was up early the next morning and was a day behind Thumper and Fixit. Caratunk is about forty miles and two big climbs away. Moxie Bald Mountain and Pleasant Pond would be challenging but the weather cooperated and I arrived in Caratunk on the second day. Actually, I missed the town which only had a few houses in it and had to backtrack a mile to the Caratunk Bed and Breakfast with its' owner Paul. The bed and breakfast had a trail reputation for great milkshakes and pork sandwiches. The next morning, I had a delicious homecooked breakfast. Leaving Caratunk, I had a short walk to the Kennebec River, where the ATC has a paid guide that takes thru hikers across the river in a canoe, because it was so dangerous to cross.

Trekking poles are amazing pieces of equipment. When I first started hiking, I thought they were just more unnecessary gear. After a few face plants, I started using a wood stick and, at some point, I invested in a pair of trekking poles. I don't know how I had hiked without them. I went through three pairs on this hike and all were in the northeast. The trail is so unpredictable and rocky that they would get stuck, bend, and finally break. I was stuck without poles once when my poles both snapped. I went to an outfitter in a ski area and they didn't have trekking poles but they had some ski poles. They are similar but not adjustable like hiking poles. They were on sale for five dollars each, as they were found on the ski slopes in the spring. I picked out two that fit me, and they lasted almost three months.

The effective use of poles could take a whole chapter. They can be used as brakes when on a steep descent by reaching farther forward. Without poles you could become a "runaway train". This happened to me when my momentum increased and caused me to lose control of my speed. I tried to brake with my poles but one got stuck in a crack and lost my grip and left the pole behind. I made a split-second decision to leave the trail and find a tree to stop me. The tree did stop me but it was with my head. Another hiker, Ponykeg was right behind me and said my head made a loud *POP!* when I hit it. I was stunned for a few minutes, but quickly recovered. Poles can also take some of the load off your legs when climbing. I've used them every day for balance and to keep my arms elevated and working to improve circulation. Most hikers adjust them shorter when ascending and lengthen them when descending.

The next seven or eight miles would be what the beauty of Maine is all about. A series of ponds and vistas that led to the Bigelow's which were a series of peaks, each one higher than the previous. This stretch is also frustrating because of "false summits". The highest point was Avery Peak and a sign at the top commemorated Avery's contributions to the A.T. With my GoPro camera on voice command, I climbed atop an old building at the peak and took a 360-degree video to remember the moment.

Wikipedia defines a false summit as, "a peak that appears to be a pinnacle of the mountain but upon reaching, it turns out the peaks summit is higher. False peaks can have significant effects on a climber's psychological state by inducing feelings of dashed hopes or even failure."

The descent from Avery Peak looked daunting. From most mountain tops on the AT, the view of the trail is obscured by the tree canopy. Not so this time, as it looked like huge jagged rocks had piled in a long, snaking line down the mountain for as far as the eye could see. The view from the summit was grandiose, but when the rush subsided, I was left with trepidation and fear. I told myself I didn't have the luxury of being scared and I'd just have to take it slow and think through every move. At this point I'm 102 miles to my next goal, New Hampshire and the White Mountains. North bound hikers have told me southern Maine is just as, or more, treacherous than the Whites. A quick look at the map with the elevations showing and it looks like an EKG of someone that needs a cardiologist. My strategy would be to take each day, each climb, and when needed, each step at a time.

Some hikers pay more attention to details like: elevations, miles, and distances to each point and place. But I just wanted to push my way to the next stop without constantly looking at a map. I tried to think more about the big picture. It's hard in Maine and New Hampshire, with their difficult terrain, to get in more than ten or twelve miles a day, and a six month thru hike would take an average of fifteen miles per day. I may be able to make up some miles in Virginia but that's a long, long way down the path.

My next trail town was Rangely, Maine. It's about fifty miles away, and there are more 4,000 footer's than you can shake a hiking pole at. I was basically hiking alone at this point as I thought I'd meet Thumper and Fixit, but I hadn't seen them. Usually there is company in the lean-to but that day I stopped early to take care of some personal hygiene. I put my things in the far corner of the shelter and took my daily sponge bath and took care of my feet. I then took care of camp chores, setting up my sleeping quarters, and filtering water. Carmen did a great job by putting variety into every resupply. I never had to eat the same thing twice in a row.

No one joined me that night. I thought I might've seen Fixit and Thumper since they had zeroed a couple days earlier, but they didn't show up. When alone in the woods, it can get a little creepy. All of a sudden you can hear every pine tree sway and every twig snap. A thunderstorm rolled in early in the morning and it didn't let up until almost 10:00 am. By the time it finally subsided It looked like I was on an island surrounded by water. When it did stop, I seized the moment and headed out slipping and sliding.

The weather improved the next few days and as the saying goes I could "smell the hay in the barn" (the barn being the trail town of Rangeley). But not before one more Hiccup. I was making a routine road crossing of which there are hundreds on the A.T. Some are only Forest Service roads and not paved but this was a highway. As I descended, I could see an opening in the guardrail on the other side. When I got there, I couldn't find the white AT blaze marking the trail or a sign anywhere. When I looked down through the opening it looked like a rockslide. At the base, I could see what looked like two trails heading into the woods. Up the road I could see a scenic overlook, and down the road was nothing. Down the rocks I went and as I approached the first trail it didn't look promising. It looked overgrown and there were no blazes marking the way. I then tried the other trail with the same results. I went back up the rocks to the highway and saw two hikers approaching the road from the trail. I recognized them from a lean-to in the "Wilderness", and we had played leapfrog ever since. I told them to wait as I already checked out the two obvious options and I wanted to look up the road a few hundred feet. Sure enough, I found a blaze leading into the woods and the AT This happens a lot on a thru hike and sometimes you can walk for hours before backtracking and finding the right way.

From the road crossing I hiked together with Graham and Flash. Flash could really motor up a mountain as he was sixteen years old and in great shape. They were only planning to make it to New York, do some sight-seeing, then head back across the pond where Flash was joining the military. They were a lot of fun to hike with.

The next morning, they were gone, and left me in their dust while scaling the first 4,000 footer. A couple days later, I came to a road crossing leading to Rangley and a night in a hostel called the Hiker Hut. It was what I'd call quaint and rustic, with small cabins, a privy, and an outside shower. The hot water and bed would be worth it. The owners were a very congenial young couple.

The husband had spent several months each year in India, helping to improve the lives of those less fortunate. When in the mountains he made silver charms with the AT logo and sold them to passing hikers. The proceeds went to help his India project, so I bought two.

My cabin had a front porch with a rocker and a hummingbird feeder hung by the door. I took some great pictures of them zooming in and out to feed. The wife offered me a beer and we sat in the yard and chatted for a while. Then she showed me her pet squirrels. She called out, and a couple came from the woods and climbed onto her hand and ate. When they were full, they took a few extra and went off to bury them.

I took a shuttle to town that evening and headed to the first restaurant I could find. My timing couldn't have been better. As I walked through the door I heard "Hey Tar". It was Thumper and Fixit sitting with Graham, Flash, Ponykeg, and Blue Dream the pit bull. What a cool surprise. We ate, drank, and made merry.

I got a great night's sleep and had some complimentary donuts and coffee at a picnic table in the yard that morning. I needed to replace some gear, so I decided to take a zero day and find an outfitter. In town again, I found Thumper and Fixit at the outfitters. They left to get on the trail and I went back to my cabin to relax. I had picked up one of Carmen's resupply packages in Rangley, so my pack was about forty-five pounds including two liters of water. I was heavy, but I was well fed and rested, so I looked forward to New Hampshire and the Whites that I heard so much about. I wanted to stop in Andover to see a hostel called "The Human Nature Hostel". There was a lot of trail talk about its geodesic dome and other features. I made it to the road that went to town and took a guess which way to proceed. I stuck my thumb out, and the second car stopped. The driver said I chose right to go to town but The Human Nature Hostel was the other way. He offered to turn around and take me back to the hostel but I didn't have cash to give him for gas so he said he'd bring me to a hostel in Andover called "Pine Ellis". When I arrived, I was fortunate enough to get their last room. Since I had tented the previous night and it had rained, I took the opportunity to dry out my gear on a clothesline. I did my laundry early the next morning, and headed to the trail head to start. Things went well until mid-afternoon, when the skies opened up with more rain.

There was a road crossing about ten miles in and I was drenched to the bone. My two biggest fears reared their ugly head again. It was about forty degrees and I began to worry about hypothermia and setting up the tent in the rain. I began looking for a place near the road to set up my tent when a car slowed up enough for me to flag him down. He offered to take me back to Andover and I gladly accepted. He took me to the Pine Ellis hostel but this time they had no room. They said they had a small cabin about five miles away and I quickly said,

"Yes". The room was a little too rustic. I cooked some camp food from my bag and cleaned up at a community restroom and shower. It wasn't much, but it was better than pitching a tent in a freezing downpour.

Up at 5:00 am, and anxious to get on the trail. Still ahead lied what, from my perspective, is the most strenuous twenty mile stretch on the entire AT The Saddlebacks are a series of four difficult mountains with false summits, ending with Saddleback Mountain itself. At that point, I would still have nearly seventy miles before crossing into New Hampshire. I loved my days in Maine, but I wanted them to end soon. It was now late July and I had only completed a quarter of the miles needed. I was looking forward to terrain I could routinely rack up fifteen to twenty miles a day and more on.

A couple days later, I cleared the Saddlebacks but they really kicked my arse. I was still standing, but barely. If McAfee Knob is the most photographed spot on the AT, then my next challenge is the most talked about. Mahoosuc Notch is touted as the "toughest mile" on the AT but first, I had to make it there in one piece. For SOBO's, the approach to the notch is a wickedly steep and treacherous descent of Mahoosuc Arm. Many times, I would stand on a precipice and think there's just no way to get down. After pulling myself together I'd throw my poles over the edge and began backing down by grabbing rocks and finding footholds. When I reached the Notch, I had a pleasant surprise. A group of hikers from my Tramily were there. Ponykeg, Obi Wan, Food Truck, and Old Bay, discussing how this should be safely traversed. We all had been warned this section should not be done alone, and now we had each other. The best description I've heard of the Notch is "it is a mile long, jumbled pile of Volkswagen sized boulders that look like they've been thrown down a mountainside. Some rounded and some flat."

So off we went. We quickly came to a point where it was painfully clear that the only way forward was through a small gap in the boulders, barely wide enough to squeeze through. We all dropped our packs and one by one we pushed our packs in front of us until someone at the other end could grab it. Onward and upward, we went until I had another of my almost daily crashes. The boulders were almost vertical, and it would be impossible to go down facing forward, as it was a shear drop. I decided the old "butt slide" was my best option, but my execution was a little lame. My foot slipped out from underneath me as I tried to get in a sitting position and *BAM*... I took the express elevator to the rocks ten feet below, landing on my rear (or what was left of it). I was afraid I'd have to be carried out as the pain was so intense. I felt I broke my hip or maybe my tail bone. My friends scrambled to my side and after a few minutes I was sore but had to go on. We finally reached a spot where we could stop and have a snack or lunch. While taking our break, we noticed Food Truck and a friend of his, both in their early twenties, had found a cave and were exploring it. They were only a little more than half my age combined. The trail community, from my experience, is a microcosm of how you wish the world to be.

Lunch is done and the rock hopping continues. No sooner had we passed a northbound couple when we heard a scream. We all rushed to the sound to find the woman's hiking partner had passed out. He was now awake, and we found out they had no water and were severely dehydrated. We all shared our water with them and told them to rest a little longer. It was a very warm July day and there was not much shade between the boulders. We made it to the end of the notch and as we entered the woods, we came across a large group of school kids. They had never seen a thru hiker, and after many questions and comments, and finishing with some posing for pictures, we were on our way again.

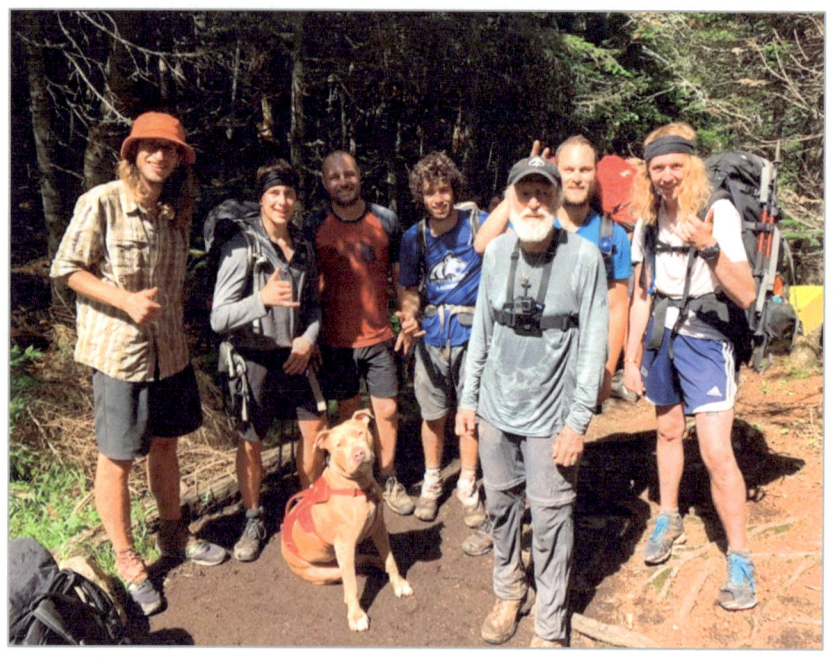

The Tramily after Mahoosuc Notch. From left to right, Obi Wan, Flash, Graham, Food Truck, Tar, Pony Keg, Old Bay and Blue Dream (the dog)

The next six miles to the Carlo Col shelter went by pretty quick, and I was getting excited as it was just a half mile from the Hew Hampshire line. That would mean, four states down and ten to go. In my readings and preparation for the hike, I developed concerns about the Whites. I learned once on the trail, that if you can get through southern Maine, you'll be able to make it through the Whites.

Roughly twenty more miles and I'd be in Gorham. I remember finding the signpost for the state line. I almost walked right by it. I guess I expected a big colorful sign, or maybe a marching band with baton twirlers and dancing girls, but there were none to be found.

Maine/New Hampshire state line

Chapter Six

New Hampshire

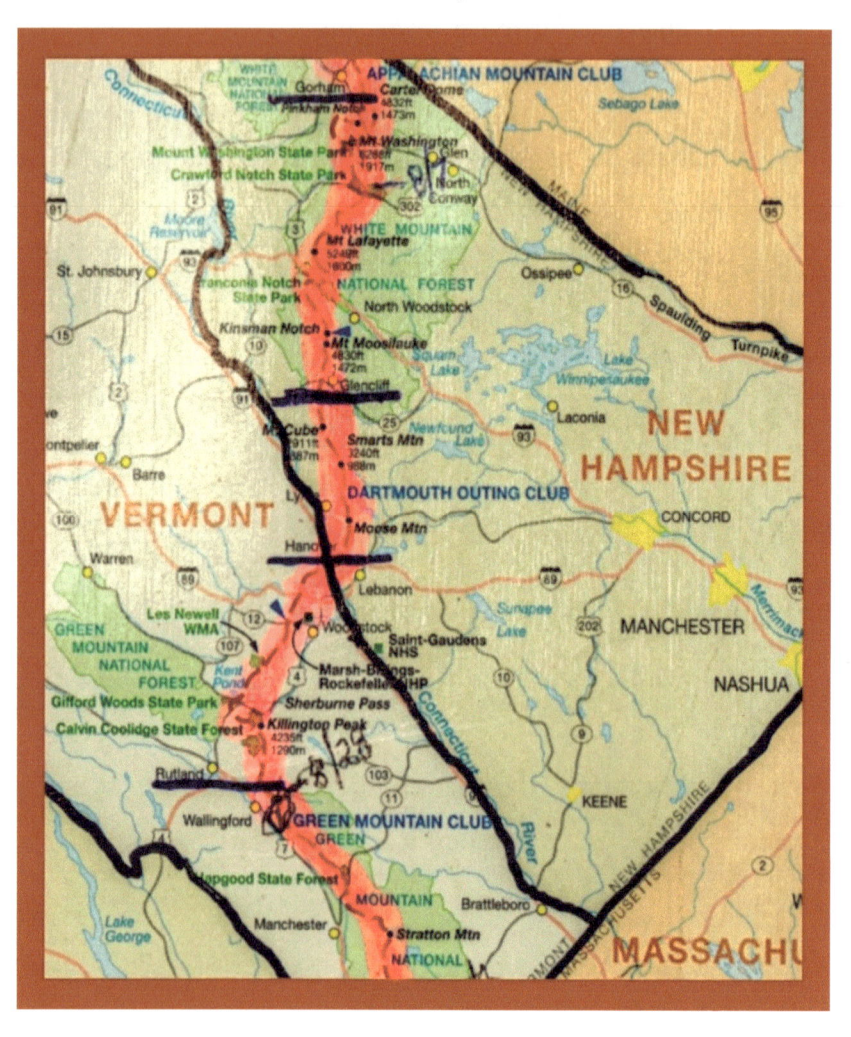

July 28, 2018

When I got to Gorham, I had about a mile walk on the road, but I wasn't sure if I had to make a right or a left. I flagged down a passing car and asked, and he directed me to town. Back in South Florida, I wouldn't recommend anyone do that, but back in the late fifties, (before air conditioning) Fort Lauderdale was a small southern town and Miami wasn't much bigger. That all changed in a hurry. Funny how the trail changes you in ways you never would have imagined.

The hostel called the "Rattle River Lodge" was a large white two-story home on the outskirts of town. It was operated by a very strict former marine. We all had kitchen privileges in a beautiful modern kitchen. Every morning they would put out the ingredients and you could cook your own pancakes.

I had another of Carmen's mail drops waiting for me at the post office, so I took a shuttle into town to retrieve it. In the morning I would be shuttled to Pinkham Notch to begin my first official slack-pack of my journey. It was twenty-one miles by trail back northbound to the hostel and I planned to do it in two days. The trail passed over a series of smaller peaks and led to the summit of Wildcat at 4,000 feet. I was on the trail early and the reduction of weight in my pack was noticeable. It wasn't exactly a slack-pack, as I was using my regular, full sized pack and I couldn't bring myself to leave my tent behind, so I ended up with about thirty pounds.

I was looking forward to my first hut visit. The hut system is pretty impressive. While doing research for my hike I found where the system was a series of large cabins with full kitchens, sleeping quarters and restrooms but no showers.

They operate off the grid, using propane to cook. They are operated by the Appalachian Mountain Club, a non-profit formed in 1886. Nonperishable supplies are packed in by the staff and helicopters bring in the perishables. There are eight of these huts and at upwards of one-hundred dollars per night, and even though it includes a full dinner and a breakfast, it is probably out of the budget for most thru hikers. They have a "work-for-stay" arrangement, where a hiker can get a meal and a roof over their head by providing some much-needed manpower. The huts vary in size and thus have different staffing levels. Small huts may only have one person working and larger huts could have five. The staffs almost always consisted of college aged men and women, well trained and pleasant. As I approached the first hut, I met Graham and Flash going the other way. They had eaten their lunch at the hut and said the staff was great.

The Carter Notch Hut was the oldest of the eight. It was still early in the day at 1:30 pm, so I intended to do the same as the "Brits" and leave for the next hut after lunch. I met the staff and I asked about the next place to camp. A young staffer took out some maps and showed me the next section was very rocky and strenuous. He said I'd be hard-pressed to make it before nightfall. I asked about work-for-stay and he said he was authorized to grant it to thru hikers that arrive after 4:00 pm or later. I then asked him if I should leave and come back later. He hesitated for a second and then said, "don't worry about it, I've got you covered." He said he'd call me in to eat after the guests were done and I'd then be assigned a chore. Once completed, you'll stack the tables, and then sleep on the floor. You just have to be gone before breakfast.

During the night as I tossed and turned on the floor, I rolled over and suddenly felt very dizzy. I rolled back and felt fine again. Later I got up for the, now standard, "Pee time" and when I stood it hit me again. I started falling but a stack of tables saved me. I battled this problem for the next ten days. Almost every time I looked up; I would lose my balance. I was told by another hiking friend that he experienced the same thing and was diagnosed with vertigo. Never a dull moment.

Up around 5:30 am and on the trail at first light. I was pumped but almost immediately the trail went vertical and covered with ragged rocks. I was poking along trying to figure out how to proceed without looking up, when I heard folks coming up from behind. I moved to the side to let them pass when I recognized them from another day back in Maine. Their trail names were Mouse Mama and O.T.B. I didn't know it at the time, but they would be joining my "Tramily". How they were given their trail names is a funny story that I'll save for later. I managed to learn to control the vertigo issue in this section. I got to the summit of the peaks leading to Wildcat and I came to a clearing with a view of what appeared to be a ski lift, but with gondolas, instead of chairs. I found out later they were gondolas, as they hauled tourists up the mountain in the summer and skiers in the winter. I sat on a large rock and ate but couldn't see any tourists. I guess I didn't know what to look for as I'm from Florida where ski runs and mountains are really scarce. It did snow in Fort Lauderdale in January 1977, but I don't remember any skiers.

I still had two peaks to conquer before Carter Dome at 4,832 feet. All had beautiful views. From there it was almost all downhill to the road crossing back to the Rattle River Lodge.

I decided to take a zero the next day and enjoy a little down time with my tramily. Later that evening seven of us sat around drinking beer and swapping stories. I remembered a night in North Carolina when another fellow hiker bought a pizza to share and I now did the same. We laughed, joked, and carried on until the ex-marine came out and asked us to break it up as we were disturbing the other guests who were trying to sleep. We were not in any condition to argue with a marine, so we went very quietly. I had to clear out the next morning after breakfast because there were no vacancies. I caught a shuttle to an RV park near town that had an upstairs bunkroom. I was joined later by Mouse Mama. We were both very anxious to get into the Presidential Range in the morning. I had prearranged for a shuttle at 6:00 in the morning so I was up early and quietly fixed a small breakfast. I got on the shuttle with Mouse Mama getting on right behind me. She said "So, you were just going to leave me behind?" I told her I didn't want to wake her. I think she was just playing with me. We would leapfrog for the next few days, then she left me in the dust as that girl could really motor.

In the back of my mind, I felt that I had two big obstacles to overcome before I could begin to make up for the time I've lost. The first being the Whites which I was halfway through, and the second was Pennsylvania. The latter was still a couple states away but I had to be patiently aggressive.

When the shuttle dropped us off at the Pinkham Notch Visitors Center, Mouse Mama headed straight for the trail head while I lingered talking with other hikers. There was a big sign board near the visitor's center with a map showing trails going in every direction. I took a few minutes to figure everything out as the sign posts were somewhat confusing. It was one of those times where I felt I might be off trail, but I wasn't sure. I wanted to get to the next hut called Madison Hut, but first I had to climb and cross the mountain with the same name. The terrain was flat and I crossed a lot of creeks, but I hadn't seen a white AT blaze in a while. This wasn't the first time I took my eye off the ball and missed the AT's white blazes. It actually happens a lot and one has to make corrections and get back on the AT. It happened to me in North Carolina and I took a nice hike back toward Georgia one time before I realized the error of my ways. These episodes will always add miles to the already large total that had to be done. This time it only cost me a couple miles but it could have been much worse.

  I was back on the AT and my ascent had begun. This will be the AT version of what is known as the Presidential Traverse. This includes seven peaks, all over 4,000 feet. They are mounts Madison, Adams, Jefferson, Washington, Monroe, Eisenhauer, and Pierce. (Pierce has been changed to Clinton). Since these peaks are so high, most of the next few days will be spent above tree line, so exposure could be a factor. It was the first week in August and it can still get pretty warm at higher elevations. I felt strong and the climb up Madison was going well, when I got to the final false summit and checked out what lied ahead. I could have sworn I was on a different planet. The entire trail was covered with boulders about half the size of the ones in Muhoosuc Notch. I could make out a speck moving up the next mountain and headed in that direction. The trail was easier than it appeared as the rocks were not slippery and it offered multiple routes. I must have chosen the right way as just before the summit I caught up with the speck I saw earlier, and it was Mouse Mama. As we stood on the summit trying to figure out how to tackle this pile of rocks, we could see the Madison Hut at the base of the mountain.

We began the descent and realized we lost sight of the AT blazes. We kept going in the direction of the hut, while searching for a white marker. Soon we found a blaze and breathed a sigh of relief. We arrived at the hut too early to request work-for-stay but we applied anyhow and were both accepted and told to wait outside for them to call us when it was time to eat. Later, four young thru hikers showed up but were declined for work-for-stay and told they could stay the night but not eat. Somehow, they ended up ahead of us in the chow line and Mouse Mama and I were left with scraps. It took me about fifty years of living to figure out life isn't always fair. My chore that night was cleaning windows and there were many. Back at Carter Notch I got to sweep the floor.

Before we could turn in that night, we were forced to sit through a presentation given by another thru hiker to the guests. It was about... you guessed it, thru hiking! My mind drifted to hours earlier when I was lying in a patch of grass outside the hut chilling out in the mountain air and enjoying some of Carmen's world class, homemade trail mix. I may have nodded off for a while, both in the grass and during the presentation.

Up the next morning in the dark, I tried to get my stove going for breakfast, but the wind forced me to a doorway of the hut that blocked the wind enough to work. Mouse Mama ate a cold and quick breakfast and then was gone. That would be the last time I saw her. She picked up her trail name back in North Carolina. When she slept in one of the shelters, a mouse found its way into her pack. The next morning, she wasted no time and packed up and left with the mouse trapped in her pack. She stopped that night and when digging in the pack found the mouse. The hikers who witnessed this promptly gave her a new name and it stuck.

If you've never heard of Mt. Washington you could google… never mind, I'll save you the trouble. It's the highest peak north of North Carolina and east of the Mississippi. The 6,288 foot peak is known for having some of the most violent weather on the planet. Winds up to 200 mph, cold rain, and snow can appear out of nowhere. That became my goal for the day. About a mile before the summit was the Lakes of the Clouds hut where I hoped to score work-for-stay again. But first there were other Presidents to conquer. Adams and Jefferson were next and although the trail skirts both summits and had side trails to the peaks, I decided to take the most direct route.

If I had to describe the Whites, it would be "rocks"… No, make that "big rocks". You know in the back of your mind that one wrong step could end the day and the hike but this has to stay in the back of your mind, as you can't be timid, but confident and focused. The signs and blazes showing the way were scarce or confusing at times. At one point in the trail I had to mentally flip a coin because the trail split and the sign had been twisted. I guessed wrong and after a very strenuous section where there were no signs of a blaze, I stopped to eat and regain my composure.

When I restarted, I had only gone a couple hundred yards when I saw two hikers below and to the right of me. They were going in the direction my gut originally told me to go. I yelled to them a couple times with no success, and on my third try they heard me. I asked them if they were on the AT. They said yes and pointed back to where I took a wrong turn. I felt a renewed sense of energy and set my sights on Washington. I missed a junction that would have taken me to the peak and I ended up at the Lake of the Clouds Hut. I crossed a road to the summit and then under a trestle for the famous Cog railroad. Built around 1900, it transported tourists up and down the mountain, a six mile roundtrip.

From where I stood, I could see the summit with several antennas and to my right looking down was the roof of the Lake of the Clouds hut. I passed a trail junction and a sign lured me onto a side trail that would take me to the top. It was only 1:00 pm and too early to check into the hut, so I followed the trail to the top. I had heard from several sources that it was heavily commercialized. I guess that happens whenever a paved road leads to a 6,288 ft. mountain top. I was surprised by what I saw next. Crowds of people and a long line of tourists waiting to take a picture with the summit sign. It looked more to me like "Disney, New Hampshire" with a huge parking lot, snack bars, and a gift shop all crowded with tourists. I received some stares as I didn't exactly look like a tourist and I probably didn't smell like one either. I'm sure I looked like a homeless ragamuffin, wrinkled and a little out of place. I made a mental note to have Carmen send an iron in my next package. Without any shame, I jumped right into the snack bar line and ordered a couple chili cheese dogs, some corn chips, and a coke.

I headed down to the hut thanking God I didn't get to see any of the weather Mt. Washington is known for. I noticed a lot of foot traffic and most were tourists wandering around taking pictures. Not all were tourists though. I saw four young backpackers behind me, and I rightly assumed it was the same four from the night before. I picked up my speed as I knew if they reached the hut first, I'd stand no chance of scoring work-for-stay. I looked back a couple times to make sure they weren't gaining ground. I heard a helicopter and watched as it touched down near the hut. I guessed it was just dropping off supplies, but I found out later it was an emergency evacuation of an injured hiker.

When I reached the hut, there was a hiker sitting just outside and I stopped and asked him if he was doing work-for-stay and he said yes. He said there were a couple others already accepted too. I went in without stopping to take my pack off and asked the crew member for the work-for-stay and he said I would be the last hiker accepted. I went back outside and continued my conversation with the thru hiker. His name was Finn and as we talked, the other two hikers we would be working with showed up. They didn't have trail names, but they would soon become Jalapeño and Haribo. I never saw the four hikers again as they either hiked past the hut or were denied the work-for-stay.

Dinner that night was fantastic. Beef brisket with all the trimmings. The crew kept pushing us to get seconds and thirds. Certain foods, like meat, can't go in a composter and must be carried out by the crew. My chore for my stay was the toughest one yet. I had to go down into the cellar and chip built up ice from the walls of a freezer. The problem was it was full of food that had been thrown in. I had to remove the food, reorganize it, chip the ice off, and a crew member came down to help me restock it. I was worn out and turned in for the night.

    My plan was to knock off (I mean climb) the next three Presidents. Monroe, Eisenhauer, and Pierce/Clinton, and end the day with Webster Cliffs. I was up early to greet a cold, foggy morning and as the fog burned off, I caught up with Finn while he stopped to take pictures. I continued on but he soon caught and passed me. Webster Cliffs were rightly named. Lots of shear rock faced drops, hundreds of feet down. The rock ledge was so narrow I thought I was walking a tightrope. I've never checked my DNA , but I'm sure there's no mountain goats in my family tree.

    I made a long descent to a road where I found Food Truck taking a break. He was heading up the mountain to Mizpah Hut a couple miles away. He then suggested I could go about seven miles down the road to Highland Center. My legs were trashed so I decided to head down the road and look pitiful enough to pick up a ride. It worked; A uniformed Forest Service guy stopped and drove me to the Highlands Center.

    The Highlands Center is operated by the AMC, and is a large complex, with four or five buildings and signs everywhere directing visitor which way to go. When I went to the big front desk it reminded me of a fancy hotel. In fact, it was a hotel with rooms that I never got to see as they were way out of my budget. The clerk said they had a bunk house, and it was available at a price I could handle. Speaking of money, before I started, I read where a completed thru hike averaged spending right around 12,000 dollars. You could spend much less if you used your tent every night and I have met thru hikers that did it. But I worked hard at a second job, saving for this hike and I wanted a few creature comforts, like an occasional bed or a hot shower or a nice big meal. I also wanted the right equipment that would increase my chance to succeed. After the hike I added my expenses, and they came out to right around the average.

Before I made it to the bunkhouse, the clerk led me to a room containing a cash bar with cheese and crackers. The bunkhouse itself had a full kitchen, dining room, living room, and a front porch. Only a couple other hikers showed up so it was a quiet night. I couldn't resist taking one more hot shower before I left in the morning. I was barely out of the parking lot when an older couple on vacation offered me a ride. They dropped me off right where I had left Food Truck the day before. I had a big climb first thing and that's the way I liked it. My legs were fresh and my mind and body were rested. My goal for the day was the Zealand Falls Hut and I arrived right at the 4:00 pm cutoff for work-for-stay. This hut was special. It had steep stone staircase about one-hundred yards long that led to the front entrance. There was also a waterfall just a few steps from the stone walkway. My work was washing large pots and pans. I didn't know it at the time, but this would be my last night in a New Hampshire hut. I was thankful for being able to stay in four of the eight.

I got off to another early start with a 4,000 foot climb to Mt. Guyot. I had a difficult four mile climb and then it leveled off but didn't get easier. Some arduous, hand-over-hand rock climbing followed. I set my sights on the Garfield Ridge shelter, about halfway up Mt. Garfield. Little did I realize that Garfield was about to hand me a mental and physical meltdown. On this very short half mile section, I must have stopped ten times. Hand-over-hand bouldering is somewhat easier because while your hands and arm are working your legs will rest. With Garfield, my hands wouldn't work, as there was nothing to grab onto and it was too steep for my poles. My legs were weak and at one point I wanted to quit or at least crawl on my hands and knees. I wiped tears from my eyes as I tried to compose myself and tell myself in thirty more miles, I'd be out of the Whites.

I reached a side trail to the shelter and I was too tired to celebrate. I just rumbled and stumbled my way to the shelter, but first I had to pay. This would be my first experience with shelters that charge a fee. Like a Hampton Inn, I had to stop at the front desk to pay. Well, it wasn't really a desk, but a tent right on the path, where a caretaker stops the hiker, gives some rules and directions, and takes your eight dollars. Some hikers disagree in principle with the fee, but for me if the shelter is newer, cleaner, and better maintained, then it's well worth the eight bucks.

Another early climb on rested legs, and I set sail for Mount Lafayette and Franconia Ridge. Lafayette was especially challenging on this day because of the weather. There were forty to fifty mph winds that were enough to move you, and since the trail was so steep and rocky, I struggled to stay on the trail. The summit offered 360-degree views and I could see my next target, Franconia Ridge. Like

Katahdin in Maine, the ridge was exposed the entire way. I passed up the Greenleaf Hut which is more than a mile off the trail. I knew I was nearing a road crossing because I began to see day hikers along the way. They were probably drawn to the well graded and gradual grade of the terrain.

The descent was happily uneventful, and I made it to Liberty Springs Campsite. No shelter here, just a few platforms that were built to create flat spots where none were found. They had what I would call a deck, plus a privy, a water source, and a covered area for cooking and eating. Caching another eight dollars and all this was mine. We managed to squeeze three tents onto one platform and since my tent isn't free standing, and I couldn't drive an aluminum stake into a slab of wood, I tied lines to large rocks I carried up from a creek. The camp was crowded, so I waited in line to cook and eat my evening meal.

The next day brought yet another strenuous hike. I guess you're as tired of hearing that as I am of typing it. But it is what it is. I wish I could start just one morning with something like, "I woke up late and a beautiful young hiker named Lola had my breakfast ready with bacon, eggs, pancakes, coffee and a special dessert she said would make me happy. After dessert, I left Lola and my pack. The trail was perfectly flat all day and the weather remained beautiful. Oh, did I mention Lola carried my pack and pumped the water for me. Wow was she ever handy." When I came to, I realized I had a dream… Not a nightmare, but a dream. There's a difference.

Back to reality… Yes, this day, like most, started with another strenuous climb. I pushed another twelve miles and arrived at the Eliza Brook Shelter about dinner time. Luckily, I snagged the last spot in the shelter. Graham and his son Flash were there already as they had passed me a couple hours earlier. Little did we know that all hell was about to break loose.

Around 10:00 pm, everyone was in their sleeping bags and the conversations slowly ended. The guy next to me began snoring so loudly, there was obviously no chance of sleeping. Graham and Flash were on the other side of the "jackhammer" (loud snorer) and a woman from Australia was on my other side. The Aussie began shouting and banging on the boards. The jackhammer would stop for a few minutes and then start again with more volume. Graham and Flash started yelling at the Aussie to quiet down and the riot escalated. At this point I climbed out of my bag, left the shelter, and set up my tent about seventy-five feet away. In no time I was sleeping like a baby. My old hiking buddy, Bob, snores but when we stop at a shelter, he sets up his tent far enough away as a courtesy to the other hikers. He says his loud snoring might be what keeps the bears away. I had seventeen miles to the town of Glencliff and another maildrop from Brown Eyes (Carmen, the real girl of my dreams). I decided to make it a two-day trip.

One more night in a shelter (Beaver Brook). It was a quiet evening as only Graham and Flash joined me. The next morning, they left early while I fixed my breakfast. I had a three mile uphill to the summit of Moosilauke, then a five mile downhill into the town of Glencliff, New Hampshire. What started as a short hike on a nice day suddenly went south. A fog rolled in before I reached the peak and the wind increased as the temperature decreased. The trail narrowed and became overgrown and muddy, so I began to think something was wrong. I stopped to look up and get my bearings and I saw a large sign that was nailed to a tree in front of me. The sign read "You are still lost". I laughed out loud and quickly reversed my course. I went back about a half mile and found an AT switchback sign I had missed. The sign in the woods saved me a long, long walk in the wrong direction.

The summit was a large bald that, on a clear day, probably had some great views, but I wouldn't be seeing anything on this foggy day. The Bald was huge and I couldn't even see all of it. The wind was blowing hard and I guessed this must be what Mt. Washington should have looked like. There were other trails crisscrossing the peak and I stopped to look at a map so I wouldn't wander off the AT again. The weather was improving so I headed down toward Glencliff.

The elation and relief I felt, having conquered the Whites was hard to describe. The rest of the day was a joy. It was a well graded, long downhill with some sections on a paved road and some on a dirt Forest Service road. I coasted into Glencliff on a high.

The Hiker Friendly Hostel was a short walk from the trail. The town was small and when I arrived at the Hostel, I noticed the post office in a house across the street. It was Sunday and the post office would open the next morning. The next morning, I'd see Graham and Flash for what would be the last time. They stopped in this town to check out the hostel. We chatted some and they were off for the trail. They were aimed at New York City for some sightseeing, then back to England. To this day I still stay in touch with them through Facebook.

I headed to the post office to retrieve my mail drop. It's a little like Christmas morning opening gifts as Carmen usually includes a surprise for me. I felt rejuvenated knowing the Whites were finally behind me. I was now fifty miles from Hanover, New Hampshire near the Vermont state line. Hanover is the home of Dartmouth College, and everything I read and heard about the area was positive.

There were still mountains to climb but they wouldn't be as high or as difficult. On my second day, on the way to Hanover, I camped in a unique shelter called "Hexacuba". Unique because it was six-sided. I shared the shelter with another thru hiker and two section hikers. There was a long side trail leading to the shelter and early on I crossed a creek by rock hopping. Then there was about a half mile uphill to the shelter where I found out the creek that I crossed was the water supply. Where's the "sign guy" when you need him. When I had to go back to the creek to filter water for my evening meal and the next morning's breakfast, I mumbled, moaned, and groaned the whole way.

This was one of the few shelters that didn't have a system to hang your food from the bears. I had trouble trying to throw a rock tied to a line over a high limb and in the process all I got was a very sore shoulder. I ended up on a lower branch and just hoped the New Hampshire bears were "altitude-impaired" and couldn't climb. I guess they were both, as my stuff made it through the night without incident.

The next morning, I was greeted with some relatively easy hiking that lasted for a couple days. The trail passed through fields and pastures which was just what the doctor ordered for my weary and aching body. I could've made it into

Hanover but decided it would've been too late, so I headed for another shelter, that was just before the town. Looking back now, I think a hostel may have been a better choice.

    The shelter was small and filled up quickly and another half dozen hiker's pitched tents around the perimeter. Everything was quiet at about 10:00 pm, when in the distance, a bright flash of lightning slashed through the sky. We all tried to go back to sleep, but the thunder and lightning crept closer. The wind picked up to the point we began to worry the shelter might come apart. The wind was blowing sideways into the front of the shelter as we all retreated to the back wall. The tenters were soaked and made their way to the shelter where we all huddled for the next 2 hours when the thing finally passed. No one slept much that night.

The sun welcomed us the next morning and I headed to Hanover where the trail soon dumped me right onto the athletic fields of Dartmouth. This was by far the coolest trail town I'd ever been through. A few days earlier, another hiker had told me there was a list of trail angels that shared their homes for free. They gave me a copy of the list with twelve or so addresses and phone numbers.

Hanover/Norwich is the first south bound town, where the trail goes right through the center. At 3.5 miles, it's also the longest road walk on the AT. My first priority was to get lodging for the night. I sat on a bench and called five of the angels on my list. All went to voicemail, so I left messages asking them to call me if they had room. Then, I waited. The trail goes right down Main Street, just like Hot Springs, North Carolina. My first stop was an Italian restaurant that had a sign saying, "hikers get a free slice of pizza." It was yummy. While there, I ran into some of my tramily: Jalapeño, Haribo, Thumper, and Fixit. Another hiker named El Gringo Loco, was also there and it turned out he was one of the soaked tenters from the night before. We all washed down our free slice of pizza with a reasonably priced beer.

My phone rang and a trail angel named Bill told me they would save a spot for me at their home in Norwich, Vermont. Their home was at the end of the 3.5 mile road walk and only a couple hundred yards from the trail. After lunch, it was time for dessert. I found a bakery that gave out free pastry to hikers. I had the biggest glazed cruller I'd ever seen. The nice waitress must have thought I looked pathetic as she gave me two more and I quickly downed them both.

I found the road to Norwich that crossed the Connecticut River into Vermont. I felt good. I completed state number five and had nine more to go. I had completed 914 miles, lost about twenty pounds, and made a lot of new friends.

Chapter Seven

Vermont

When I arrived at Bill's house, no one was home. So, I just hung out and waited. In a short time, I got a call from his wife Betsy. She said she was on her way home from work and would be home shortly. I thought that was very considerate of her. One other hiker showed up, and Bill and Betsy invited us to join them for dinner. After the meal, she took a minute to tell us there would be no charges for the lodging, food, or laundry which she so graciously did for us. She told us how her son had a medical emergency while hiking and was taken in by a family. The family refused compensation but asked they "pay it forward". Bill and Betsy took it to heart and they not only started taking in hikers but recruited others to do the same. This was the list I was given a few days earlier. At the end of her talk, she asked us to do the same and pay it forward. She then gave us a sticker with their name and address and asked us to stay in touch to let them know what we did to advance their cause.

I was up and going at first light with a backache from the air mattress I slept on. I planned to make it to Rutland, Vermont in four or five days. Thru hikers affectionately refer to Vermont as "Vermud". The reputation was accurate as there were hundreds of boardwalks through the bogs of mud. Some sections had no way around it so you just had to plow your way forward. The uphills were especially trying as one had to spend more energy and effort to navigate the path. It was August, and it was very hot and humid. Even though it was draining me, there were bright spots with beautiful views and waterfalls.

Hiking was smooth and fast except for the occasional mud, so I made good time. I was near a road crossing that led ten more miles to Rutland. It's not really a trail town, but I had heard some good and bad things about a shelter there and wanted to check it out. I made it to the road and put on my "please help me" face and I had a ride into Rutland in two minutes. My ride found the Yellow Deli hostel and dropped me off. A woman at a shelter a couple days earlier trashed the Yellow Deli as a "cult", and other hikers said, "it was like an old hippie commune without the drugs." The building looked like an old boarding house or hotel; three stories tall and right in the center of town. I entered and someone told me to have a seat in the waiting room. When he came into the room, he greeted me politely and took a few minutes to go over the rules which were about the same as most hostels. He then took me on a short tour and showed me my bunk assignment. After a welcomed hot shower, I went down to the restaurant on the first floor and had a delicious, fresh, organic meal.

That evening I took a walk (yes, you read that right) into downtown and found a little bar. The patrons all seemed to know each other so I had a couple cold ones and returned to the hostel. For whatever reason, I felt lonely and missed my family. In the morning I awoke to another bad back episode. I had trouble straightening up, so I decided to take another day to rest and hopefully ease the pain. The pain continued and I was at a low point thinking, "maybe I should bag it up." I could handle the physical pain but the difficulty sleeping was beginning to take a toll.

I knew the negative thoughts had to get out of my head. I thought about all the people that donated to the American Cancer Society in my name to honor my son and sister that were taken by the disease. And I thought of the promise that

I made to my mother in her last days. She told me I had to finish what I started and I told her I would. That was enough to get my head screwed back on correctly. I decided to get a haircut at a downtown barbershop and when it was over, I felt better about myself and the hike. I had taken too many zeros, and lost three weeks in Florida with my mother, and every day I'd start doing the math. I'd been hiking for four months and I still hadn't made the halfway point. That meant even if I had smooth sailing the next four months, it would be December in the mountains of Virginia. Talk about a challenge. I decided to "just do it" as the Nike shoe salesman would say.

When I returned to the hostel, they were leading a new hiker through his tour. It was Big Sky, the hiker I met on my second night in Georgia. He seemed preoccupied and said, "I'll catch up to you later". He never did and I never saw or heard of him again.

I stopped at the bus depot in town and checked the schedule. A bus left the depot in the morning and would bring me to where I could pick up the trail where I left it. I was determined to start hiking whether my back hurt or not. Mt. Killington was in my way and I headed right at it. I heard there was a cabin near the summit and after a while I started looking for it. When I did find it, I was disappointed to see a dilapidated stone and wood structure with broken windows and the door falling off. I've stayed in worse, so I stopped. There were ski trails crisscrossing all around me but all were quiet, being the last week of August. I was only a quarter mile from the summit, where there was a ski lodge and a snack bar

I'm now officially in the Green Mountains of Vermont. Not only that, but the trail signs now say AT/LT. The LT being the Long Trail, with 273 miles in Vermont. The AT follows this trail for one-hundred miles before splitting off. The LT is the oldest trail in America, dating to 1918.

Appalachian Trail/Long Trail sign

Trekking the next few days were fun. I passed NOBO's almost every day heading to their Katahdin celebration. There were a lot of stream crossings and boardwalks to avoid the always present mud. I arrived at a shelter and decided to spend the night as it was a nice setting with a stream and plenty of campsites.

I sat at a picnic table, unstrapped my pack, and took out some snacks. I was there for five minutes, when two young college age guys came up and we began to talk. They didn't have packs on, so I knew there was a nearby road crossing.

They both had expensive looking cameras hanging around their neck. One said they were doing research for a school project and asked if they could get some pictures of me. Lucky for them I got that haircut in Rutland because I was beginning to resemble either the "Unabomber" or "Charles Manson". We had a long conversation and they took their pictures and left.

More hikers arrived and the rains began to fall again. We didn't get the thunder and lightning, but a steady rain kept us in the shelter until dark when everyone drifted into some stage of sleep. Another hiker showed up and was greeted by those still able. He sat down and it looked like all he had was a small daypack. He said he was trying to break the "unsupported speed record" for the Long trail. He rested for about fifteen minutes and was gone. He was back in a few minutes because he couldn't find the trail. I always prepare for my next day by knowing where the trail is. If I'm up early, it's dark and hard to navigate.

I took him back out (in the steady rain) and got him on his way. The next morning, I aimed for the Green Mountains and had a planned stop in Bennington, Vermont. Leading up to Bennington was Stratton Mountain. It wasn't exactly rock climbing, like I faced in the Whites of New Hampshire, but more like climbing endless stairs. When I finally broke out of the trees and reached the summit, I found a ski lift and a small building. I sat on a lift chair and had my late summer lunch at a winter playground.

I wasn't alone long before I noticed a guy with no pack walking toward me. I correctly figured he was one of many that wanted to know answers to questions like "any bears today" or "what do you eat", etc., etc. After a brief show and tell, I excused myself and ran to get back on the trail. I usually didn't take sit down breaks to eat, as it would always take a few minutes to loosen back up. On my way out I checked out the building and it was unlocked. A note on the wall welcomed hikers and said they could use the building as a shelter if needed. It was very small and would only hold two or three hikers max. I thought that was a nice gesture.

I looked all over for a white blaze and finally found one. It ran straight down a ski trail. It made me think about what happened if winter hikers happened to be here as crazed skiers crisscrossed the slope dodging hikers. I passed a few more hikers from my NOBO bubble that day. Since I restarted in Maine, I was now a SOBO and I had hiked and met a lot of great friends, but I really didn't have a SOBO bubble.

I had some equipment problems with my hiking poles and attempted to fix them. The poles had taken a lot of wear and tear and were bent instead of straight. I tried to straighten one and it just snapped. I saved the two pieces and limped down the trail with one pole.

Before I arrived at a shelter that night, I passed a couple setting up camp a hundred yards before the shelter. I found an old concrete platform with an old-fashioned water pump in the center. I figured it was from an old homesite years ago. I went over and pumped it but no water came out. It did make some loud pig-like squeals that could have awoken the dead. On the path to the shelter, I passed an empty tent, so I guessed I would have company. The guy noticed my broken pole and offered to help me out. He disappeared for a minute and came back with two poles he said were left in the shelter.

He had to work with the poles to get them to adjust but he did it and I was back in business.

The couple returned around dinnertime and we enjoyed some more time together. I was alone in the shelter that night. I had another episode of my recurring stomach problems. I woke up with severe nausea, put my headlamp on, and headed to the privy area. I never made it that far but I did empty my stomach somewhere on the side of a very dark trail. I guess it was some bad food as I went back to the shelter and slept like a baby.

My next shelter was Stratton Pond located next to, surprise! a pond. This one had a caretaker, but when I passed his tent no one was home. I figured he was out doing trail maintenance or something. The shelter was new and spotless with a grill and several picnic tables. A couple was sitting at one of them and I stopped to chat. They said they were section hikers and had stopped at a nearby town to pick up a few snacks, beer, and hamburgers. They then invited me to their little cookout, which I quickly declined... Yeah right... I accepted. While the party was in full swing, the guy said, "Look down by the pond, that's the thru hiker that hikes in his 'tighty whiteys'". I looked over my shoulder and sure enough, there he stood. We had a good laugh as the exhibitionist trekked past the pond. This was trail magic at its best. Food, drinks, and live entertainment. Before returning to the shelter, I walked to the privy to clean up and take care of business. This was a ritual that I followed whenever possible.

I may have gotten my best night's sleep yet. I was ready to go early and had lunch at the next shelter. There, I found three friends from my NOBO bubble. One of them was not one of my favorites as I knew him to be a cheater. The AT works on an honor system, but we all know not everyone has honor. The name given to these so-called hikers is "yellow blazers". One that I met was very proud of his cheating and would tell everyone how he could beat the system. What bothers me the most is they call themselves thru hikers. I don't reach up and touch each white blaze, but I walk every mile and with side trails, detours, and a whole lot more.

New England rock wall

    I stayed in a shelter fourteen miles from Bennington, Vermont where I had a maildrop from Carmen waiting for me. Unfortunately, I didn't get much sleep. A character wandered into the shelter wearing a cotton t-shirt, cowboy boots, and no pack or water. He seemed harmless and fell asleep leaning on a big rock.

I climbed into my sleeping bag when another late arrival that I had seen before, wandered in. She was either British or Aussie and was very loud. Most hikers are considerate in camp, but she wasn't like most hikers. She decided to "cowboy camp" in front of the campfire that was still burning. Another hiker with a similar lack of consideration decided to join her by the campfire where they both loudly laughed and talked until after midnight.

When morning came, I ran out of the shelter. No coffee, no breakfast, just a Cliff bar and I was gone. I raced down the trail without falling once and improved my AFPD (average falls per day) to just under two… I just made that statistic up so don't bother to look it up or google it… When I reached the highway, I wasn't sure which way the town was. I was about five miles away from town and had heard there were no hostels, but there was a hiker friendly hotel called the Catamount. I couldn't call as there was no service on my phone. I met a guy leaving a barn and I asked if I could use his phone, but he had the same service I had. He helped me out the best he could by pointing in the right direction to town.

As I walked toward Bennington, it wasn't long before a car stopped. When I told the driver where I was headed, he said, "Get in". A few minutes later he dropped me off at the front door at the Catamount motel. The manager checked me in and was very helpful by showing me how the town was laid out. He also said the motel offered free shuttles to the trail. I decided to rest a little and get a long, hot shower and then go out to find some hiker food. (Cookies, Fritos, Snickers and ice cream. It's all about calories)

It was a Saturday, and the post office was closed. That meant Carmen's mail drop couldn't be picked up until Monday, causing me another zero I couldn't afford. I think it was here where my ice cream addiction really kicked in. It became a necessity to fill up with a pint or more at every trail town. Even with an ice cream habit, I was still down twenty pounds. I like to think this tasty, frozen habit is a medical emergency. Sometimes I'll even wash it down with a cold beer.

Sunday turned out to be a busy day. I took a short walk, found the bus depot, and took the bus to a local Walmart for some resupply and to check some gear since there were no outfitters in town. When I returned to the motel, I decided to wash some of my gear as the sun was out and I could get the items dry. I filled a bucket with soap and water in the bathroom sink and started scrubbing my tent and my backpack when I realized I had no way to rinse everything. I ended up bringing everything into my room and rinsing my gear in the shower. I spread the tent on the lawn and hung the backpack on a light post in the sun to dry.

As I looked at my pack hanging on the pole, I was reminded of a night many miles away in North Carolina. **The shelter was full and after 9:00 pm, it was quiet when some one on the upper level turned their headlamp on and it was followed by a loud thud. Everyone's head popped up to look, and the guy with the headlamp on said "I saw a mouse on someone's pack, so I threw my boot at it." His light went out and everyone nodded off. The next morning, I realized it was** *my fault as I'd left a half empty bag of trail mix in my pack that night. The mouse apparently survived unscathed.*

First thing Monday I headed to the post office, picked up my mail drop, emptied it into my pack, and caught the shuttle to the trail. I had eighty more miles to go to reach Great Barrington, Massachusetts. Like the other states, Vermont wasn't going away without a fight.

The first day on the trail was uneventful and I arrived at a shelter to see a half dozen hikers hanging around, laughing and joking, so I introduced myself and joined them. Before long, my trail friends from Maine joined us. Most of these people were day or section hikers so it was probable that they wouldn't be observing Hiker Midnight. Fixit and Thumper were equally nervous, so we set our tents up a short distance from the shelter. We used the amenities at the shelter to prepare our meals and eat and then returned to our tents.

I crawled into my sleeping bag, hoping to get a good night's sleep, but it wasn't to be. Around 1:00 am, I woke up with indigestion. The sweaty palms and dizziness meant I was probably having another episode of something I was diagnosed with fifteen years earlier. It was called Vaso-Vagal Syncope, and I knew what came next. I'd soon pass out and have a seizure. I found a suitable tree that I could hug in order to prevent a fall. I slowly lowered myself until my lights went out. I woke up a while later and returned to my tent and sleeping bag, feeling like I had dodged another hike-ending bullet.

The next day was rough. It either had something to do with the previous night's episode, or I was just tired of the Vermont mud. The last mile of every day always felt like three miles, but today it felt like ten. I was so trashed; I was literally crying out loud. But then I wondered, if you're crying in the woods and no one can hear you, are you really crying at all? Maybe not.

I rested well that night and was on the trail early the next morning. I was quickly rewarded with a sign that said, "Welcome to Massachusetts". As usual there were no marching bands or dancing girls, but I ran into to state tax collectors that demanded payment for entering their State.

Chapter Eight

Massachusetts

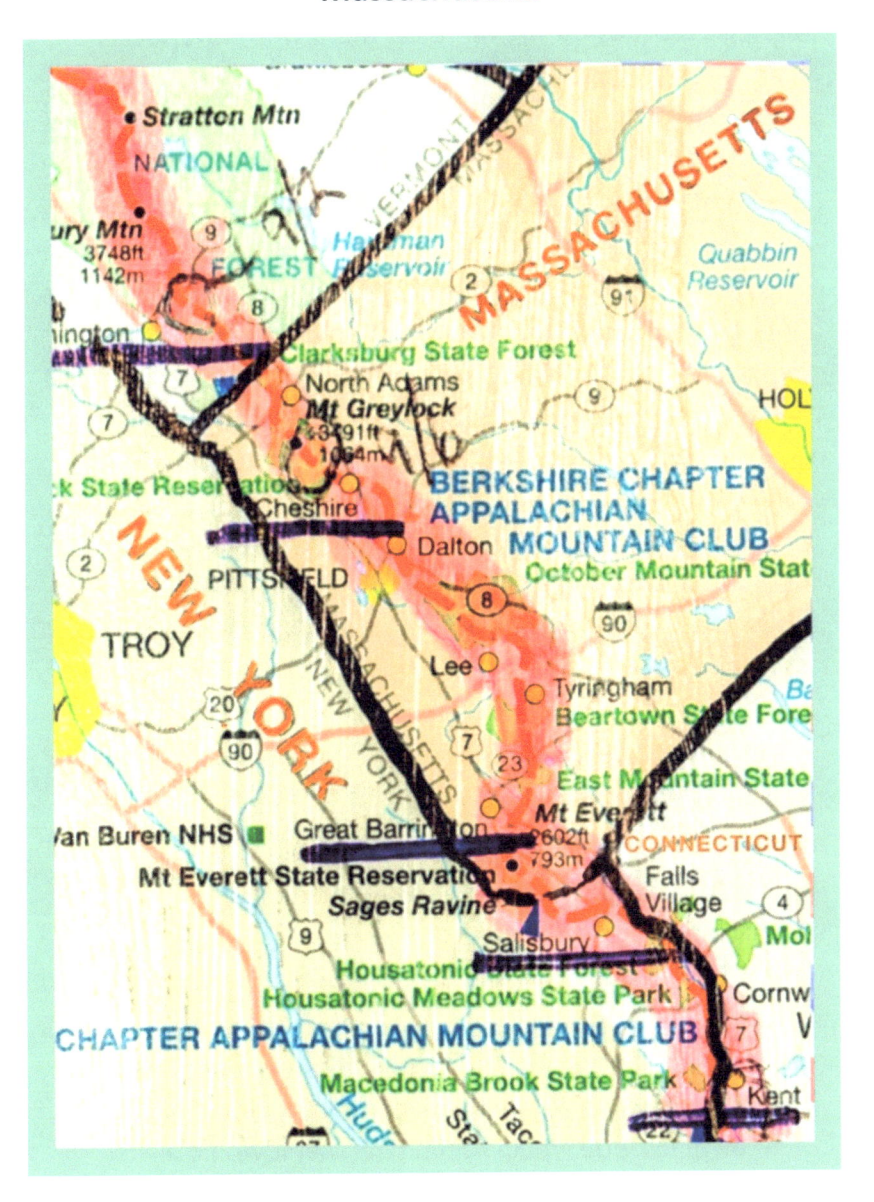

September 6th, 2018

Next, I aimed for the town of North Adams, Massachusetts. It was the first week in September and still in the high eighties during the day. The lower elevations were even warmer. I was saturated in sweat when I came upon a camping platform, so I stopped to dry off and have some lunch. I peeled off my soaked shirt and hung it on a branch. Then I thought, "What the heck" and I took off the rest of my clothes and hung them with my shirt. I was nervous and kept an eye out for peeping whatevers. About that time, I heard a dog bark. I jumped up and yelled, "Hold on, I have to put on some clothes". A female voice shot back, "Okay". I got myself reassembled and let the hiker through. I hoped she wouldn't rename me "The Streaker".

In my hurry to get dressed, I forgot to put on my prize possession, the GoPro camera I wore on a chest harness. I returned to hiking and walked three miles before I saw it was missing. It was too late to make it back before I'd run out of daylight. I made a decision to get a room in North Adams, then return to try to find the camera.

I yogied a ride back to the hotel and when I retrieved my pack from the back of the truck, I saw my GoPro hanging from my backpack. A needless detour that could've been worse. I took a short break to calm down and then made a beeline for the trail and the next shelter.

My next goal was a town called Cheshire. I heard of a Catholic church in town that allowed hikers to tent in their yard and use the facilities in their community hall. From there it would be a two day hike to my mathematical half-way point of 1,100 miles. Bob would remind me that it would all be easy and downhill from here. If he were with me on this hike, he would've whined and moaned and groaned the first 1,100 miles and been happy and celebrated "going home" for the last 1,100.

The hike to Cheshire took me over Mt. Graylock, the highest point in Massachusetts at 3,900 feet. The summit held a beautiful War Memorial Tower and a big fancy lodge accessible by car. From the peak, the rest of the day was a gradual downhill with easy hiking. I reached a road and spotted a Dollar General store. I had time, so I went in and bought a few snacks. I'm sure the locals that saw me sitting at the curb stuffing my face with junk food figured a new homeless person had showed up and they were partly right. Hikers are homeless people with money.

I found the church and a note on the door that had a number to call to have the door unlocked. He showed up quickly and welcomed me. I had access to the bathrooms, and he gave me directions to the local restaurant, where I had a delicious dinner and a beer. I returned to my tent at the church and met some new friends. Curtis was a thru hiker and Denise was doing a section with him. We would hike together for the next few days.

The next morning, I left the church and promptly headed a half mile in the wrong direction. I figured it out, righted my course, and caught up to Curtis and Denise when they stopped for a lunch break. We got back on the trail and Denise sprinted ahead. "She must be one of those speed hikers", I thought to myself. It was only about nine miles into Dalton and when I got there, the trail ended at a big parking lot.

The trail became the highway into town. I passed a bronze AT marker embedded in the concrete and AT blazes on the light poles led the way into town. The town was typical quaint New England with neat homes and gardens. One home I passed had the biggest sunflowers I'd ever seen. I stopped to take pictures, but when I saw the pictures later, they didn't do the flowers justice.

I reached the center of the town and met up with Curtis. He said Denise had traveled to another town to replace some gear. Curtis and I found a pub and had some lunch with a beer to wash it down. He made contact with Denise, and said he heard of a place in town where a guy let hikers pitch a tent in his yard. We found the place and the owner (I think his name was Paul) laid out some rules. Rule number one was, 'no one was allowed in his house for any reason.' He apparently had been burned once and he was now overly cautious. Another hiker showed up that I recognized, it was Food Truck. He asked Paul if he could set up his hammock on the front porch and Paul agreed. That night I found an ice cream parlor in town and was able to get my fix and satisfy my new craving.

The next morning, Paul had a great breakfast all set up on a picnic table. Coffee, tea, muffins, etc. We thanked Paul for his generosity and headed to the trail head. As soon as we made it, they all took off leaving the old man and his forty-pound pack in the dust. I began to worry my trail name may be changed to Tortoise. The day matched my pace, overcast and gloomy, a bad omen. Food Truck and I leapfrogged all day as the weather went downhill into a steady downpour. We both made it to the Wilcox shelter just before dark. I did something I rarely do and asked Food Truck if he could set up my air mattress and sleeping bag as I was wet, cold, and worried about hypothermia. I changed into dry clothes and by that time, he had me all set up. He did it without hesitation and I always tell him he saved my life that night.

There were two shelters in this place, one was older, and they were about 200 yards apart. I found out the next morning that Curtis and Denise were in the other shelter. They passed me on their way to the trail. We caught up later in the day and hiked together across the Massachusetts Turnpike on a pedestrian bridge. Next was a climb on a well graded climb to the Upper Goose Pond Cabin. This was another very unique experience.

Upper Goose Pond Cabin, Photo taken by Amelia Cary

The cabin had two levels. The upper level had a bunk room and a small private room for the caretaker. She was a gracious and very helpful woman. Downstairs was a great room and a full kitchen. Curtis took charge and cooked dinner for everyone. We all went to bed with a bellyful of spaghetti. The caretaker had breakfast ready the next morning. The pancakes hit the spot but I felt bad that I couldn't tip because I had no cash.

Great Barrington Massachusetts was about twelve miles away, and we must have been flying because we arrived just in time for... breakfast! (again). There were no hostels in this town, so Denise said she had enough and headed home while Curtis, Food Truck and I split the cost of a room at a Days Inn. After a long search we found a laundromat and cleaned some of our clothes.

Where Vermont had mud, Massachusetts had greased rocks. Not really, but one morning I slipped and fell five times. I was ready to call one of those lawyers that I've seen on TV that handle "slips and falls". I think it had something to do with the trail always being damp and wet, and the rocks get slick from moss and fungi. I was approaching Connecticut where I was born, and I hadn't been back in about fifteen years. This time I told myself there would be no marching bands to greet me and sure enough I wasn't disappointed.

Massachusetts/Connecticut state line

Chapter Nine

Connecticut

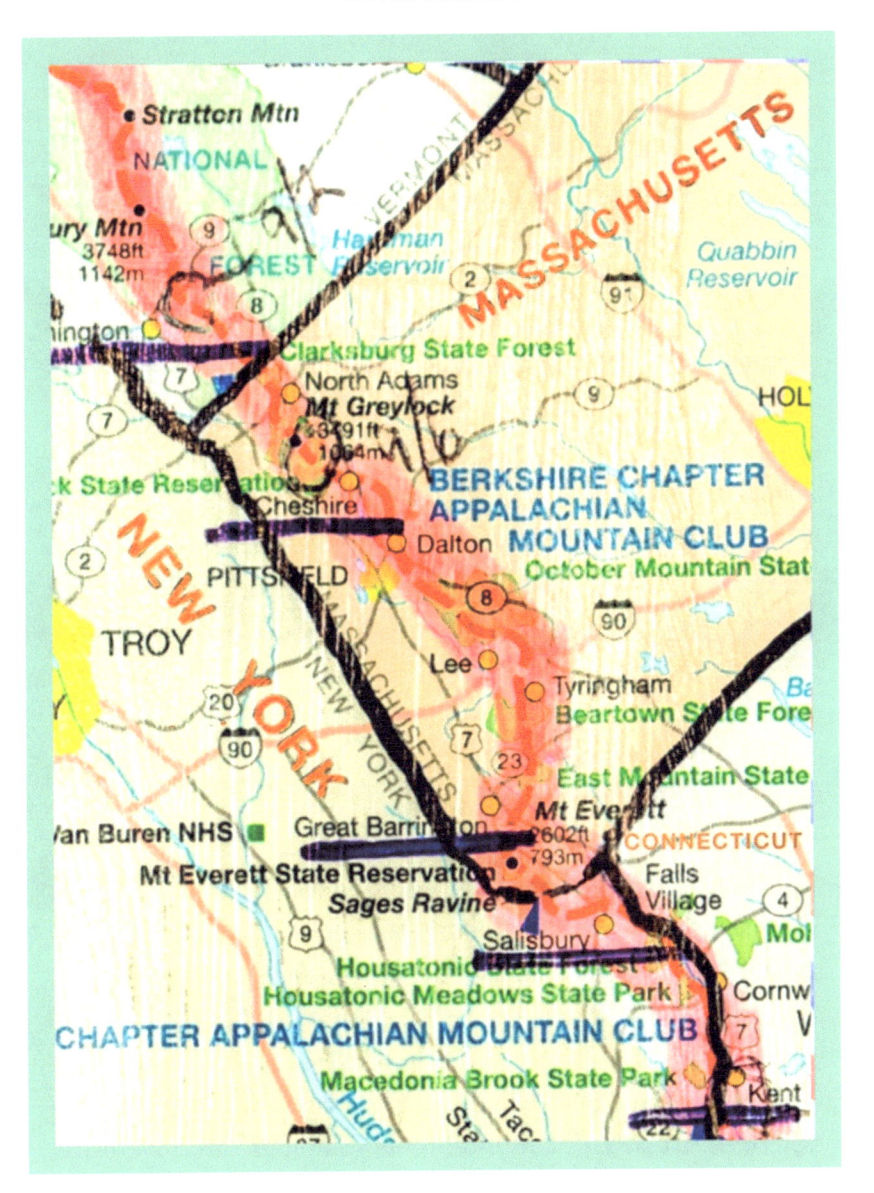

September 14th, 2018

I strolled into the small town of Salisbury, Connecticut and did some quick math. I had completed six states of the fourteen needed, but winter is coming, and I'm not used to, or real fond of, snow and ice. Curtis and I looked for a place to sit and relax and could only find an upscale bar and restaurant. It wasn't in a hiker's budget, but it was all that we could find. We went in and the bartender was really friendly. He let us sit and nurse a couple beers and he even found some snacks for us.

Curtis knew of a place to spend the night, so we went looking for the address. It was a lady's house not far from the town and when we arrived, there was no one home. We went around back and saw a sign on the back porch welcoming hikers to make themselves comfortable. We did, and after a short while, a woman came to the back door and showed us to our rooms. The owner was in the hospital with a broken hip, but she had her neighbor keep the house open for hikers. This is what's so beautiful about the trail. It restores your faith and trust in the love that surrounds us. On this day, I was proud to be Connecticut Yankee. We had the house to ourselves and after a hot shower, we headed back to town to find a reasonably priced dinner.

We ended up at a ramen noodle restaurant. A lot of hikers eat these on the trail, but they have a lot of sodium, so I try to avoid them. These were not the packaged meals and were very good. It was a pleasant evening and we returned to the house.

As I laid in bed that night, I was filled with anticipation for the next day. For months I had planned this adventure, looking over maps and searching for ways I might meet up with old friends or relatives. The first was with my friend Bob back in Georgia and North Carolina. Second, I had circled Kent, Connecticut, where my nephew and his beautiful wife Diana and their two daughters lived.

Curtis and I were up and ready to start the next morning when I realized one of my most important items was missing. I searched hiking magazines to find the best down-filled jacket I could. With my aversion to cold, I didn't worry about price but I wanted quality. I remembered I had it at the ramen noodle place and must have left it on a chair. The question was, would it still be there, and would the place be open this early? Curtis and I had our breakfast at the house as there were a stock of items for hikers to use. We then headed to the noodle restaurant. When there, I tried the door and it was locked. I decided to tell Curtis to go on and I would wait however long it would take. I told him I would check the back door. I went back and knocked loudly, but no answer. I was heading to the front to tell Curtis to go on without me when someone yelled from behind me. I told the guy my sob story and he went back in to look. He returned in a couple minutes with the jacket and I thanked him. I was happy that I dodged another bullet and didn't have to waste any more time, money, or energy.

Kent was thirty-two miles away and I wanted to make it to a shelter halfway there. Time seemed to fly as the terrain was easy. Some of the trail follows the Housatonic River. We passed a huge park, then over the river near a hydroelectric plant. I began a climb when I heard the unmistakable roar of race car on a road course. I knew of a track in Connecticut called 'Lime Rock', and I wondered if this might be it. I reached a cut in the woods where I could see the racetrack below. There was also a hang glider launching point in view, and I thought it was interesting as I never saw either of these anywhere else again.

When I reached Kent, there was a short road walk into town where I found a convenience store at an intersection. I went in and found some snacks, and then found a spot with some shade. I called my nephew, Scot, and he said he'd meet me soon. Because of this stop, I never saw Curtis again.

The next few days were just what the doctor ordered... Family. I'm not articulate enough to express the deep sense of comfort and relaxation I felt. Scot's wife, Diana, and I spent a day together (Scot had to work). We stopped at an outfitter and went to downtown Hartford where I grew up. We even visited Saint Peters Church and School where, at seven years old, I attended school and sang in the choir. Later that evening, we went out to dinner as a family, which was better than I could imagine. I loved my trail family, but this was so much better.

Scot has always been a sports car enthusiast. His success in the business world allowed him to get involved in racing.

He was very proud of the Porsche race car that he and his brother built and raced. I really wanted to stay, but old man winter was hot on my tail, so Diana drove me to the trail head and after an emotional hug, she was gone, and I was standing there with... no hiking poles!

After thoughtful consideration, I decided to get on the trail. I texted Diana and told her not to worry, I would pick up a pair in the next trail town. A short while later, Scot texted me back and said he was looking at maps and would drive out and meet me at a point where he could park near a forest service road and walk up to meet me. I found a branch in the woods and fashioned a hiking pole. The timing for the meet up was perfect and I got to see Scot one more time. Thanks Scot!

Chapter Ten

New York

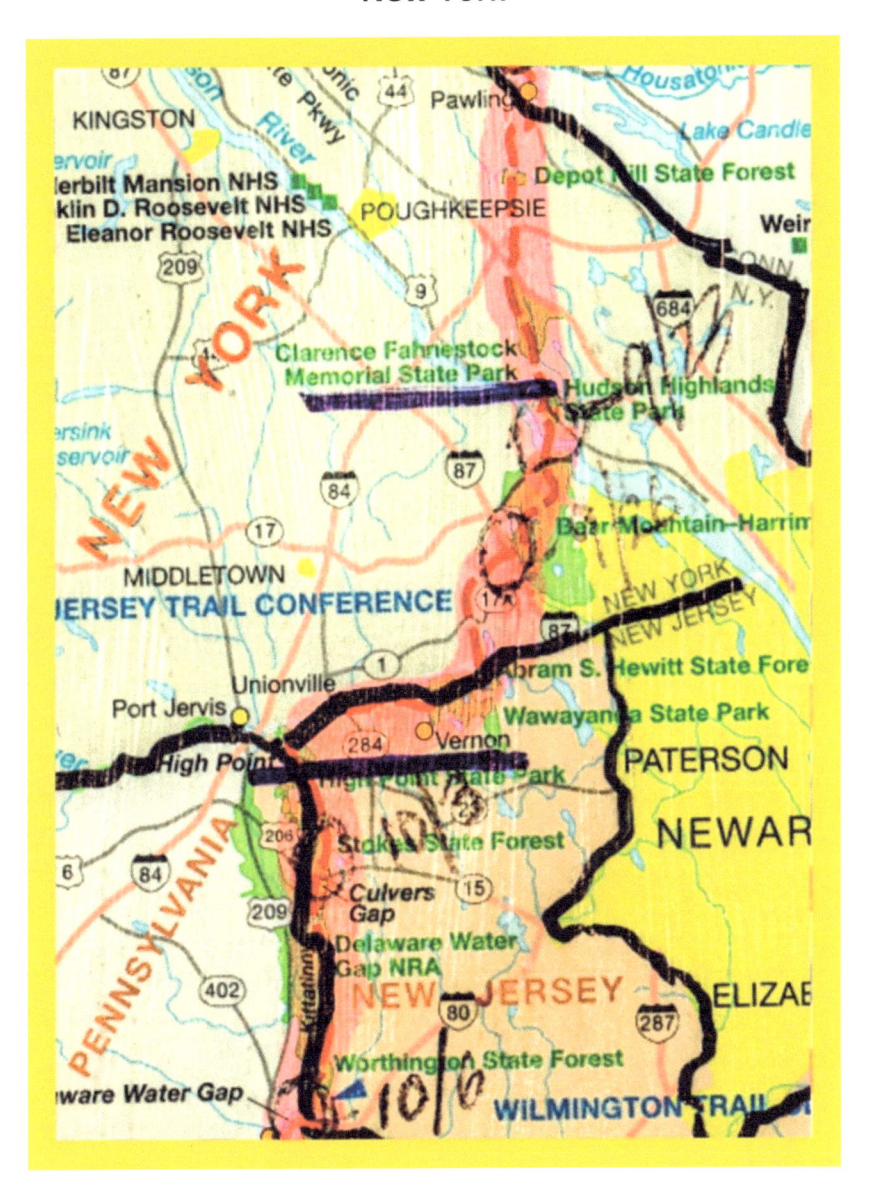

September 20th, 2018

Well rested and with fresh legs, I was flying high through farms, fields, and meadows approaching the Connecticut and New York state line. I glanced over my shoulder and saw a body closing in. My runner instinct kicked in and I picked up the pace. I stopped at a road crossing and tried to find where the trail continued. The guy behind me caught up to me. I didn't know him and he said he was section hiking. Neither of us could find the trail, so we guessed and went left.

In about a quarter mile we found it. It was an old train station. Yup, right on the AT sat a depot with a sign above it that said, "Appalachian Trail Station". I found out later that a commuter rail line still runs to Grand Central Station in New York City. My new friends' name was Thread. He said there was a deli about three quarters of a mile up the road and he convinced me to join him. We had a big breakfast and waddled back to the depot where he took off up the trail like he had a rocket up his butt.

The significance of this story is that my good friend Sunshine, who had successfully completed an AT hike over ten years ago, was an inspiration to me for my own hike. I found out later that she was visiting New York that very day. She decided to hop a train and ride the sixty-five miles to the Appalachian Trail Station and check out the trail. We probably missed each other by minutes. But then maybe I saw her and the way my brain had been working, I didn't recognize her.

A couple days of smooth sailing and nice weather forced me into making a decision. There was no shelter close enough and it was late in the day. I could stealth camp or take a green blazed trail to Fahnestock State Park. The sign said it was 0.2 miles away and it seemed longer, but I finally made it to a beautiful lake and after finding directions to a cleared field reserved for tent camping, I pitched my tent near a picnic table and was soon joined by Thread. While he was setting up, I took a walk to see what facilities the park had. The park was closed for the season, but one restroom was left unlocked. It even had a shower... A cold shower but beggars can't be choosers.

It didn't rain during the night, but it may as well have. Morning brought a heavy fog with an equally heavy dew. This was one of the camp chores I hated the most. I had to take my pack towel, shake the water off the tent and then begin wiping it dry. It's worth the effort as wet tents and equipment can add a lot of weight to an already heavy pack. I was only looking at a twelve mile day, so I took my time and had some breakfast.

I made it back to the trail and had planned to see one of the few places that I had circled on my "must see" list. As a child growing up in Connecticut, my parents were devout Catholics, and my Dad was a member of a lay ministry called the third order of Saint Francis. The Franciscan order of Priests had a monastery in upstate New York called Greymoor, and my father would attend a retreat there every year. On one occasion, I either rode there to bring him or went to pick him up. I'm not sure which, as it was about sixty-five years ago. I do remember it made a huge impression on me. I also remembered the drive up a winding road that, at the time, seemed to me as big as Mt. Everest.

Why on earth was I so surprised that my visual image of the place was so different from the reality only sixty-five years later... duh. It changed from a tiny little monastery to a megacomplex of dorms and conference buildings. Oh well, they still had a place for a weary hiker.

The Greymoor Spiritual Life Center as it is now named, is a half mile road walk from the AT. Nearby was a deli/convenience store and here began my "Deli Blazing" (a hiker term that refers to eating at every available deli within walking distance of the AT). There were many of these stops in New York and New Jersey and this one would take care of my dinner and tomorrows breakfast.

A big reason we can enjoy the trail

Morning brought more heavy dew... Oh well... some more wiping and wringing and I was on the road looking for the trail head. After a day of PUDS, I arrived at the west end of the Bear Mountain Bridge. This iconic structure was the longest suspension bridge in the world when it was completed in 1924. Almost a hundred years later it's 2,200 foot length still looked impressive. The trail crosses the bridge and when I reached the other side, I had caught up with Thread again.

Thread and I reached a park. We walked through a tunnel and past a playground, and we ended up at the base of Bear Mountain. There were 1,100 steps of hand-hewn granite that led us up the AT to the summit. Even though it was their slow season, there were a lot of sightseers and day hikers walking around. The summit held an observation tower and we couldn't resist. There were maps, photos, and historical information on the walls and I took too much time, but I had to read it all. The top had an observation deck and it said New York City could be seen on a clear day. Well, it wasn't clear, and I couldn't hang around waiting for better weather.

I was getting cold, so I told Thread I was heading to a shelter five miles south. He was going to make a phone call and catch up to me. I headed off Bear Mountain and then after an uneventful afternoon, started climbing up West Mountain. I thought the shelter was near the top, but I never saw it. I did see a side trail but there were no signs. I kept going and started the descent when I stopped for a moment to consider my options. I finally realized that I'd passed the shelter as it was 0.6 miles off the trail, so I decided to go on instead of backtracking. I started again and I thought I was making good time when it occurred to me, I hadn't seen a blaze in a while. It was getting late in the afternoon, but I felt confident I could make it to the William Brien Memorial Shelter before dark. But it wasn't meant to be. I came to a clearing in the woods to see a million cars passing. It was the Palisades Parkway at rush hour and there was no way I could cross it at this hour. I walked back into the woods and found a flat spot that I could squeeze my tent into.

I needed water and remembered a small stream a short distance back, so I made a beeline for it. It turned out to be more like a muddy trickle, so I skipped the water, put on my headlamp, and headed back to set up my tent in the dark. Setting up a tent in the dark is no easy task, but after staking it into rocks and a tree it was ready. I ended up with Carmen's delicious trail mix and a Clif bar for dinner. There was no easy way to hang my food bag, so I stuck it in the vestibule of the tent and prayed there wouldn't be any critters sniffing around.

9/11 memorial flag painted on the trail

My plan was to be up and out early as there was a shelter a mile down the road with a water source. But for now, I needed some sleep. No sooner did I crawl into my sleeping bag when it started raining. The rain beating down on the tent put me right to sleep. I woke up at 2:00 am and it was still raining. I was concerned about flooding, so I put on my headlamp and looked around outside. Everything looked okay, so back to sleep I went. It didn't last long as I felt a kind of urge that I hated to get when it was dark and raining. I had to "go", and it wasn't going to wait. I was unsure what to do, so I took all my clothes off, put on my boots and headlamp, grabbed some supplies, and ran down the trail into the woods to complete the task. Mission accomplished, I streaked back to the tent, dried off, put on my dry clothes, and crawled back into the sleeping bag. It was about forty degrees, but I warmed up and ended up sleeping pretty well.

I was up at 5:00 am and it was still raining. At 6:00 am, I heard footsteps walk by and I guessed it must be Thread. It had to be, because I never saw him again. I'd been in and out of this tent for ten hours, but I couldn't bring myself to leave. I decided to wait out the rain and at 8:00 am, after thirteen hours, the rain stopped. I packed up my gear and made it across the Palisades Parkway safely. I'd only been half a mile in when I found a big, clean creek where I was able to pump enough water. I drank until I couldn't drink anymore, then sat on a rock and fixed some breakfast.

I set my sights on the New York/New Jersey state line coming up in thirty miles. My friend Sunshine in Florida told me about the "Lemon Squeezer" on the trail in New York. When I reached it, I saw she had described it perfectly. There were two large slabs of granite about eighteen inches apart. Most people would probably take off their pack to squeeze through, but I thought I could make it and I did with both sides scraping the granite.

A couple days of easy hiking and well-spaced shelters, and I crossed into New Jersey. That's nine down and five to go. I had a mail drop in Warwick, New York to pick up. Yes, the trail hugged the New York/New Jersey line and I planned to hitchhike into the town. I met two young female hikers and after brief introductions, they said they were waiting for an Uber. I asked if I could split the fare and share the ride and they agreed. They dropped me off at the post office and I found that I had made it there before my maildrop. I had to spend a night and hope the package made it the next day.

New York/New Jersey state line

Chapter Eleven

New Jersey

September 30th, 2018

The girls I shared a ride with were leaving the trail because one was injured, so they gave me some of their leftover trail food since they had no need for it. I found an inexpensive hotel and walked a mile to check in.

The next day I walked back to the post office and my package was there. I tried to figure out how to get back to the trail. It was about ten miles and there was no buses and no cabs. I realized the girls may have had the right idea so I decided to try Uber or Lyft. I'm not that tech savvy but figured I'd give it a try. My first attempt failed, but my second attempt worked perfectly. I celebrated by going out to dinner, then I hit the sack.

The next morning was cold and raining and Uber delivered me to the trail head. The weather got better but the trail got worse. Boulders, rocks, and more boulders. I met a woman with a group of children out for a walk. I knew there had to be a road crossing somewhere and sure enough I stood on a road with a sign not far away that said, "Ice Cream, Apple Pie and Fritters". That was all I needed. Ice cream had become my favorite trail food. I gorged myself because I knew I only had two miles to go until I'd be at another one of my circled meetups. This was where my stepdaughter and her daughter were going to meet me.

I passed through a muddy cow pasture and a short trail before I got on the Pochuck Board Walk over an ancient lakebed that was now a swamp. The boardwalk cost was 30,000 dollars and was one and a half miles long. Lynda and Emily were to meet me at the end, and I was looking forward to some hugs. But it didn't work out that way. No one was there so I called Carmen and she was able to find out that they couldn't make it.

Tight butt cheeks on this part of the trail

I yogied a ride to the nearest town and got a room for the night. In the morning, I took a cab back to the trailhead and disappeared into the woods. After I passed the Pochuck shelter, the trail followed the New York/New Jersey state line, kind of like the trail in the Great Smokey Mountains National Park follows North Carolina and Tennessee. The trail began a steady uphill to the High Point Shelter, but before I reached it, I came across a young couple. The girl was sitting on a rock with her shoe and sock off. I asked her if she needed any help and they declined saying she could make it to the shelter. The last half mile was very steep but it had several switchbacks to ease the pain. I had company in the shelter, and I was the only thru hiker, so I had a lot of interesting conversations.

Misty Lake

The young couple tented and there were no snorers to interrupt my sleep. The remainder of New Jersey included miles of bog bridges (Puncheons), a lot of pastures and some small rock climbs. I met another hiker going North Bound that stopped to warn me about what I was heading for. He said the summit I was heading to was overrun by motorcycles. When he asked them why they were on protected land, the designated leader of the pack answered, "My father owns this mountain, and we can do what we want." I thanked the hiker for the heads up and continued the climb. When I reached the top, I wasn't surprised, but shocked. Ten or twelve motorcycles on the rocky summit all stared at me like I was an alien. I returned the look but bit my tongue. The leader told them to move out of my way, which they did. I reported the incident to the AT headquarters in Harpers Ferry when I got there. The next thing I noticed was something written in white paint on the boulder I stood on. It had "N.J." on one side and "P.A." on the other side. Another state line and I would be in the land of rocks for the next 230 miles.

Chapter Twelve

Pennsylvania

October 6th, 2018

I now have Pennsylvania, Maryland, and West Virginia until I get to the big one (Virginia). I still have over 500 miles to do in Virginia until I reach Damascus, where I stopped my north bound hike when I heard the news of my mother. I knew I had to keep putting one foot in front of the other and it's not getting any easier. The weather is catching up to me and it is getting colder each day.

I was nearing my planned destination of the Mohican Outdoor Center when I saw a sign that said, "M.O.C. 0.3 miles". I had read about this place when I planned this section and had it set for a maildrop. It was run by the A.M.C., they are same group that operates the huts in New Hampshire, so I expected something rustic, but I was pleasantly surprised. When I walked in, there was a gift shop and a mini outfitter. A young man checked me in and asked if I was hungry. I doubted any thru hiker ever answered no to that question and I wouldn't be the first. He led me to a seat in the dining room and said he'd fix me something. Holy Moly... I didn't expect this at all. He returned with some food, a key, and directions to my cabin. The cabin had a full kitchen, a living room and two hallways with private rooms on each side.

I was told I wouldn't be able to pick up my maildrop until the next day when the manager came in. Another unavoidable zero day. There was nothing I could do to speed up mail delivery, so I decided to try to get a good night's sleep. In the morning the manager told me the mail was still in the post office and she would pick it up when she made her daily trip to town. The package reached me in the afternoon and I restocked my pack and boxed up some of the stuff that wouldn't fit and marked it for my next stop. I brought it back to the M.O.C. office and asked if they could forward it and charge my bill with the postage and they said they would.

I wasn't alone that night as I was joined by Troop Leader. He was a former Army Ranger and he picked up the trail name, "Troop Leader" somewhere on the trail. He was also a flip flopper like me and was heading to Harpers Ferry to complete his thru hike. We ended up hiking over 300 miles together and I could fill a book with our adventures. He had some great character traits. He was polite, congenial, and an excellent conversationalist. Not a big guy at about five foot and nine inches tall and 155 pounds, about the same as me. He always had a big grin and usually had a wad of tobacco behind his cheek. I'm guessing he was about twenty years younger than I. He wore a vintage looking world war two German infantry cap. I never asked why but assumed he just liked the looks of it. His hat had an unhappy ending that I'll cover later.

We hit the trail together in the morning, but he had a light pack, and liked to hike fast for the first half of the day. He would usually disappear in the morning and I'd catch up at lunchtime or early afternoon. On our first day, we made it to the Delaware Water Gap. The name of the place always intrigued me. A Water Gap is a complicated phenomenon and to oversimplify it, flowing water over millions of years, cuts a path between a couple mountains. It was a sight to behold as in some stretches it was as much as four city blocks wide. The Delaware Water Gap is part of the river of the same name.

We crossed the bridge over the river and halfway across was another white line painted with "N.J./P.A.". Yes, we were in New Jersey again. This happens along the hike fairly often.

Troop Leader and I made a decision to call it a day, so we left the trail for a small nearby town. Unfortunately, the only hotel had big, out of a hiker's budget, prices. Troop Leader got on his phone and found a better priced hotel in neighboring Stroudsburg, and a call to Uber got us a ride to the door. We both got a shower and headed out. He was looking to get a haircut and I was hungry as usual. I had a philly cheese steak and a couple beers and we walked back to the hotel.

For the next few weeks, we would dance our way through "Rocksylvania", as it is known to hikers. It wasn't big rocks that destroyed so many hiking boots, but the small, jagged, pointy rocks that covered the trail, leaving almost no flat spots to plant your foot.

Eckville Shelter, photograph taken by Sarah Jones Decker

One night in the first week in Pennsylvania, we had to tent at a campsite because the next shelter was out of range. The wind was gusting and the temperature was dropping making it hard to set up a tent. Frozen fingers don't work well. We had to backtrack a mile on the trail to find a weak trickle to pump water from. We were both happy to put that night behind us.

The next couple days were almost flat hiking and we were making great time. Then came a great example of how you have to constantly adapt to change on the trail. We had planned all day to stop for the night at a place called Smith Gap, where the trail crossed a road. There was a restaurant/bar and grill we were looking forward to. When we made it, the parking lot was empty and the doors were locked. There was a phone number on the door and Troop Leader called it. The owner answered and said he would be there in a few minutes. He said if we could help him lift a heavy grill into his truck, he would give us a few beers on the house. On the house was our favorite beer, so we hoisted the grill into his truck and sat down. He gave us a beer each and proceeded to tell us about how he had run the place for a couple years but was not able to make it profitable, so he closed the doors two days before we got there.

Troop Leader and I sat on the front porch trying to come up with "plan B". We talked about different options but there was always something wrong. Troop Leader then got on his phone, found a nearby trail angel and made the call. He said he'd pick us up and we could sleep on the floor in his garage and we could shower in his house.

There's a popular saying on the trail that says, "When things get rough, relax... the trail will provide.", And so it did for us on this day. The trail angel was John Stempa. He drove for half an hour each way to get us and bring us to his home. He brought us into town to a restaurant where the beer was free with the dinner. The next day it was raining hard, so we both took a zero and John took us into town where we did laundry and had breakfast.

The next morning John drove us to the trail head. John was a true angel and a great conversationalist. He loved to brag about his son, the rock star who, with his girlfriend, played in a local band that was very popular in that area.

As I put my pack on and started adjusting the straps, Troop Leader was disappearing from sight. He sure had a lot of early morning energy. It doesn't matter whether it's a brother, a sister, a wife, or a friend, just because you want to hike together, doesn't mean you'll agree on the same start time, pace, miles, lunch, pee stops, or anything else. Troop Leader and I had different styles, but at the end of the day and most of the afternoons, we were together. I think we both made concessions to our styles so we could enjoy the hike together. Splitting the cost of hotels, and hostels, and helping each other made the trail easier for us both.

I caught up with Troop Leader just before Lehigh Gap. This place had a view that resembled a mini Katahdin. The view was beautiful but since you had to rock-hop and carefully watch every footfall because of what looked like a massive rock slide across the ridge, one rarely had a chance to sightsee. We then found a small rock outcrop that appeared to be a perfect viewpoint, but was occupied by two pack-less guys that looked like they were going to be there a while. We rightly assumed there was a road crossing nearby. They greeted us with a dire warning about the trail ahead. It went something like this... "You won't believe what you're coming up on."

Lehigh Valley in "Rocksylvania"

In a matter of seconds, it became painfully clear. A nearly vertical descent filled with huge boulders. At first I was scared, and this wasn't exactly my first rodeo. I had to stop every few steps to figure out which way was the least likely to end my hike. We made it through somehow without breaking any bones, but It's times like this that I liked hiking with someone who, if need be, could direct the medivac helicopter or identify my body. I actually felt safer crossing the busy road at the bottom of the descent. The next stretch was a 0.6 mile ascent to the Outerbridge Shelter. We had just started the climb when Troop Leader raced ahead again. He usually stayed close at the end of the day, but he must have felt some of that morning energy. I caught up with a young couple that wore sneakers and no pack. They must have left their car on the last road crossing and they decided to walk on the AT for a spell. I was getting close to the shelter and I saw a water source, so I stopped and pumped some so I wouldn't have to backtrack later.

Troop Leader was waiting for me at the shelter and we both went about setting up camp. Shortly after dark, we hit the sack but kept on yakking and, like the new generation, playing with our phones. Speaking of the newer generation, I haven't noticed too many out in nature, playing, hiking, or anything else that doesn't involve the constant use of opposable thumbs. Right on schedule, here comes two athletic young men of the new generation. That is, actually in the woods and using their feet, legs, lungs, and brains. Troop Leader recognized them from another place, and it turned out they were speed hikers in the purest sense. They were both fun guys, laughing and joking and you could tell they weren't bragging when they talked about their twenty-five to twenty-eight mile days. They would "stop and smell the roses" another hike, but this was more of a run and about speed.

I was up at 5:00 am and they were long gone, leaving without making a sound. No breakfast, just up and out to the next stop. I think I could give them a run for their money if I was just twenty years old again, but like the celebrations every time I crossed a state line, It ain't gonna happen. We never saw them again, but Troop Leader may have stayed in touch with them. I'll have to ask him. Troop Leader and I have talked on e-mail since his hike ended in October 2018, and It was great to hear from him.

During the next few days, we passed over the knife Edge, which is a long section of peculiar boulders that are flat and pointed. Navigating it was to be a challenge. The pinnacle was interesting but way too close to a road crossing with a lot of available parking, that meant lots of tourists and day hikers. Mind you, that's not necessarily a bad thing, but the peace, quiet, serenity, and solitude of the mountains was one of the main reasons I had to do this hike. At 1,700 feet, the pinnacle was said to have some of the best views in Pennsylvania, but an overcast day wouldn't allow long range views.

Not "The Pinnacle", but a beautiful view
I came across on the trail.

That evening, we arrived at a shelter to find two tents spread end to end blocking the entrance. The shelter could hold eight to ten people, but the entrance was closed. We figured they saw there were other hikers needing to get in and would clear a path, but no, they just stood there. Finally, Troop Leader had to say something to them, and only then (after finishing their beer) did they get up and break down the two tents. They then dragged out a big cooler full of beer and carried it up to their vehicle parked a couple hundred yards away. I wasn't surprised when they didn't offer us a beer.

Troop Leader loved his campfires and he never missed an opportunity to build one. This night would be no different, and it turned into a beauty. A couple overnight hikers stopped and asked if we'd share the fire and we said, "sure". That was a mistake because they could sleep till noon and still be back at their car at 1:00 pm. They stayed up until the last embers died out and we were left with three or four hours of sleep. It's hard to put in fifteen miles with only four or five hours of sleep, but whenever you camp near a road, it can and sometimes does happen.

We had smooth sailing for the next fifty miles, but it was now mid-October, and I passed my 1,500 mile mark. I'm worried about old man winter, but all I can do is keep pushing south and hope I can stay ahead of the worst of it. I'm now a "Florida Cracker" (not by birth, but by my sixty-five years of residence) and I can't picture myself walking in snow or ice.

We were now approaching the town of Duncannon and the Doyle hotel. Thru hikers nearly all bring this place up as a must see, when discussing Pennsylvania. When we were fifteen miles outside of town, Troop Leader said he was going on ahead and if I didn't see him at the shelter in five miles, it would mean he headed for the town.

501 Shelter, photograph taken by Sarah Jones Decker

When I arrived at the shelter, he wasn't there so I knew he felt good and continued on. The shelter was one of the nicer shelters I'd found. It had a loft and an alcove with a picnic table. As I finished setting up my bedding, a section hiker rolled in with two beautiful blue-eyed Huskies. The first thing he did was sit down with the dogs and began picking ticks off them. This was something he had to do every day and he'd pick as many as thirty off of each dog every day. He vowed not to put the dogs through it anymore and would be hiking alone after this section.

I knew I had a short ten miles into town where I hoped to meet up with Troop Leader. I was up in the dark, quietly fixed breakfast and was on the trail at first light. The last few miles before I descended to the Susquehanna River were a joy because the trail followed a ridge with numerous views of the river valley. I must have stopped ten times to see the views and "smell the roses". On the descent, I ran into a middle-aged lady who was hiking up to the ridge. I answered a lot of her questions about thru hiking, and she said she wanted to do it someday. I offered her encouragement and she went on her way.

When I got down to the highway, I crossed some railroad tracks and the road. The trail followed over the river on a bridge then made a left over another smaller bridge. I called Troop Leader and he said he was glad to hear from me and would pick me up in a short time. He had run into an old friend with a motor home in an RV park near the river. We visited, ate, and drank a few beers. With a full belly and a little buzz, we put on our packs and walked about a mile to the Doyle.

With a rich history, the hotel was built in 1770 and burned to the ground in 1803 and rebuilt. It was purchased by Adolphus Busch in 1880 and has become a tradition among thru hikers. The couple that owns it now are friendly and down to earth. Their restaurant and bar are very low key and the food was delicious. Later that night, I found an ice cream shop that satisfied my craving until the next stop.

Troop Leader and I met for breakfast at a little diner across the street and when we were done, we headed to the trail. After a steep ascent up Cove Mountain, the terrain became easier and we started making good time. We entered the Cumberland Valley and it seemed like forever to get through. The trail went in a stairstep fashion almost all the way across the valley floor.

As we entered Carlisle, Pennsylvania, we completed an eighteen mile day. We decided to take a cheap motel that was just down the road. We stopped at a gas station and had a hot dog and bought a six pack of beer. The next morning, we had a continental breakfast at the hotel and headed off to the trail head. What happened next was really special to me and a highlight of my journey. My sister Anne Marie was in Pennsylvania visiting her oldest son and his family. She was following me on the satellite tracker I wore and knew we were close, so she wanted to meet up with me. Wow, that made my day.

We made tentative plans to meet at a road crossing on Route 94 outside of Boiling Springs at about 5:00 pm. It was a seventeen mile day, but I was pumped and that wouldn't slow me down. We hit the ATC regional office a little before noon, had a nice chat with the staff, and picked up a few souvenirs. After a quick lunch we were back on the trail again. I was able to reach Anne Marie and she said they should be there on time. Troop Leader and I made it to route 94 about fifteen minutes late but there was no sign of Anne Marie and her husband Larry.

It was beginning to get dark so we decided to head into town and hope they would find us. Troop Leader went ahead as I stopped several times trying to get a signal on my phone without success. The road had no lights, and all of a sudden everything was dark except for head lights. I had to walk next to the road and the cars and big trucks were flying by. A truck stopped and offered me a ride but I was worried that if I got in, I might miss my sister.

I finally got a text that said they were trapped in a huge traffic jam. When I got to an intersection, Troop Leader was there waiting for me. In about thirty minutes, Anne Marie and Larry rolled up and Troop Leader and I jumped in and started to warm up as it was getting cold. My sister had made arrangements at a hotel in Carlisle. Troop Leader and I began laughing as we had just walked all day from Carlisle.

The hotel she picked was a huge upgrade for us. We had a nice dinner, and in the morning Anne Marie and Larry dropped us off at the trail head. She gives great hugs. Mom must have taught her that. Troop Leader took off again and was soon out of sight. I figured I'd catch him at Pine Grove Furnace State Park, which was ten miles away. This park is the home of the "Ice Cream Challenge". This is another thru hiker tradition that has been going on for thirty-five years. The challenge is to eat a half gallon of Ice cream in one sitting at the general store in the park. The reward for completing the challenge is a wooden spoon that say's "Member of the ½ gallon Club". Word has it seven out of ten hikers left with the spoon. I'm pretty sure I'd leave with a spoon in each hand as I had been training for months. When I arrived, I found the store was closed for the season.

I caught up with Troop Leader at the shelter that night and we were joined by a woman with red hair. Her name would be easy to remember... it was Red. Like us, she was a SOBO thru hiker. The next few days we hiked together... sort of. She could really motor, so we didn't always hike together but would usually meet up during the day or at a shelter. We hiked together on and off for about a week but she was fast and next thing we knew, she was gone. I would see her again in a few days, and I kept up with her through texting while I was still in Virginia, she was in North Carolina.

On the first full day, the three of us hiked together, we stopped at the Quarry Gap Shelter. If there had been an award for best maintained and aesthetically pleasing shelter, this place would win it all. Most shelters are just what you'd expect: rough, rustic structures made of logs and stone. This one was painted inside and out, landscaped grounds, potted hanging plants, and had a nice covered area for eating or socializing. It was too early to stay, so we reluctantly left for the trail.

The next stop was unplanned as I pulled up lame in a place called Fayetteville. There was a Walmart in town and we planned to pick up some supplies and get back on the trail, but the pain in my foot became bad enough to cause a limp. I thought it best to get a room and rest my foot for a night. I hoped it was only a pinched nerve and would be better in the morning. It was three or four miles into the town and we were lucky enough to get a ride from the third car that passed by. Of all the hitches I made on the hike, this was the only woman that stopped. She may have been attracted to the "Unabomber" look I was sporting, but she didn't say.

I ran into Red at the Walmart as she was leaving. She was returning to the hotel that was right behind the store. She said her parents were in the area and wanted to visit for a while. We got together later in the evening, and it turned out her parents brought her boyfriend to surprise her. What a great family.

During one of our previous shelter stays, I had told Red that there was only one side trip penciled in during my adventure and that was to see Gettysburg. I loved American history in school, and to see Gettysburg was always a dream of mine. Her comment that night was, "Maybe, I can arrange that". That evening with her parents she brought it up and they said they could work it out. It was about twelve miles away from where we were in Fayetteville. The next morning, her parents dropped Troop Leader and I off at the trail head where we had a fifteen mile day to highway 16, where Troop Leader had made a reservation at a cheap hotel. The miles got my foot aching again.

We checked into the hotel, cleaned up, and headed for the nearest pub for grub and brew. On our way back to our room, Troop Leader got a call from Red and she said that they wanted to come by early the next morning and take us to Gettysburg. I was stoked. We were back in the room for a minute when Troop Leader realized he'd lost his hat. "I must have left it in the pub", he said as he headed out the door to retrieve it.

When he returned, he was not a happy camper/ hiker. No one had seen the hat at the pub and he wasn't his happy self all evening. I thought the worst. Maybe a World War II vet or a vet's relative helped the hat disappear because it was a German hat. My father was a marine on Guadalcanal and for the rest of his life he wouldn't buy anything made in Japan. Troop Leader wasn't in the mood for conversation, so I started checking out my trail maps. It looked like we were so close to the Maryland state line, I could throw a rock there.

Morning came quickly and we all piled into Red's family car and headed to Gettysburg. It was even more than I expected. It was a cold rainy day so we spent almost the entire time inside the museum. With thousands of artifacts, video's, and interactive demos, there was enough to see in the museum and we really wouldn't have been able to stay any longer. It was a great experience and I'll treasure the memories. In the morning we took a shuttle back to the trail head. Red stayed behind to spend more time with her folks and I never saw her again, but we still stay in touch.

Just a few miles left of Pennsylvania, and only a few days out of Harpers Ferry where Troop Leader and I will part. We've been together for all of Pennsylvania and I'm not looking forward to hiking alone. The next few nights were interesting. One night we met a new hiker who was on his first hike to test new gear. He said he'd like to do the thru hike, so we knew there would be a million questions coming, and there were. He was hiking back to his car the next day, so we pretty much stayed with him. Troop Leader had already scouted out the trail guide and found a hostel at the next stop.

When we arrived at a road crossing where the new guy's vehicle was parked, he asked us if we needed anything and we asked if he could drop us off at the hostel. He said, "sure" and we threw our packs in his trunk and we headed to the hostel. Troop Leader called the phone number and got a message saying it was closed, starting the day before. Oh well, now to plan B. It was now raining steady so we made our way back to the trail and headed for the next shelter. We made it before dark and met a caretaker that lived in a house behind the shelter. He told us of an Italian restaurant nearby that would deliver to the shelter. Troop Leader called the number to order and it was closed for the season. We broke out the camp stove and cooked something up. The Maryland state line was coming up and we crossed it the next morning.

Troop Leader 'leading' the way in a cornfield

Chapter Thirteen

Maryland & West Virginia

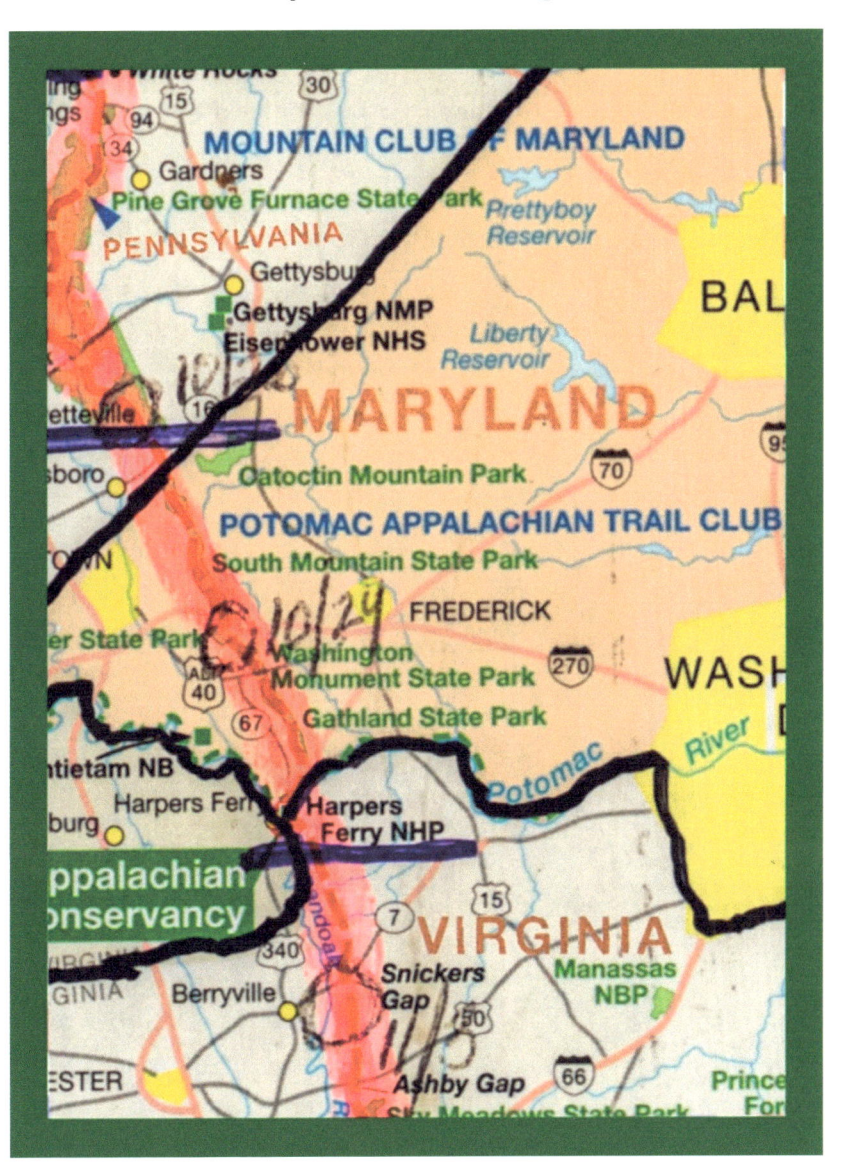

October 26th, 2018

Maryland is the home of Thumper and Fixit, whom I hiked with for miles in New England. I hadn't heard from them in a while, but the trail gossip said they were still hiking ahead of me.

Maryland's forty miles flew by and before we knew it, Troop Leader and I were half a day from Harpers Ferry at the Ed Garvey Memorial Shelter. It had an enclosed loft with windows and a view. We didn't go inside because it sounded like a young couple that apparently couldn't afford a real room were in there giggling and more. We chose not to interrupt the love birds and we moved on

Ed Garvey Memorial Shelter hosting the lovebirds.

In the morning we headed the short distance to Harpers Ferry. It's the headquarters of the Appalachian Trail Conservancy and the traditional (not geographic) halfway point in the hike. Troop Leader had mixed emotions as his hike was down to a few miles. I'd have the same feeling someday but not today. The walk to Harpers Ferry was great. The last few miles were along the historic C&O Canal Towpath. Because of my love for history, these last few miles were especially fun for me. We climbed up the railroad trestle and crossed the Potomac River. Just thinking about General Washington crossing the same river with his rag tag army in the dead of winter almost 250 years before gave me goosebumps.

After the obligatory high fives, we set about exploring the town. We were chomping at the bit to get to the A.T.C. headquarters. Over the years I had formed a mental image of this iconic place and it turned out just like I had envisioned and maybe more. When we did the traditional sign-in and photo in front of the A.T.C. sign on the front of the building, I realized it was an experience I would cherish for life.

I started scanning the pages of the visitors' log looking for my tramily and friends that had gone before me. I thought to myself that some may still be in town and sure enough, as we were hanging around the A.T.C. up walked Pony Keg and Food Truck. I said something about going back to the hotel and he said he just got there and he wanted to hang out for a while. I didn't know it, but he was stalling me as he'd called Thumper and Fixit to come back. They had left earlier that day and when Pony Keg called, they came right back. What a cool surprise that was!

Troop Leader and I in front of the ATC headquarters

We made the most of our reunion and went out to dinner with a large and somewhat scraggly group. We partied and swapped stories all night and as time went on, some got a little rowdy and being it was Halloween night, wanted to go trick or treating. Troop leader and I headed back to our room, as I had to hit the trail the next morning. Little did we know, the party continued until the wee hours.

In the morning, I had mixed emotions and second thoughts. A part of me wanted to stay with the friends I grew to know and depended on to keep me moving, motivated, and entertained. It was going to be hard to walk away from Troop Leader, but he completed his mission and it was time for him to go home.

I still had 550 miles to go and the calendar page now says November. I wasn't sure how I would make it, but I knew I had to hurry. Troop Leader walked with me and started the steep but short ascent out of Harpers Ferry, West Virginia. We had an emotional goodbye, or at least I know it was for me. I was tempted to look back from the summit, but I didn't. The state line came up quickly and I found myself in Virginia again.

West Virginia/Virginia state line

Chapter Fourteen

Northern Virginia

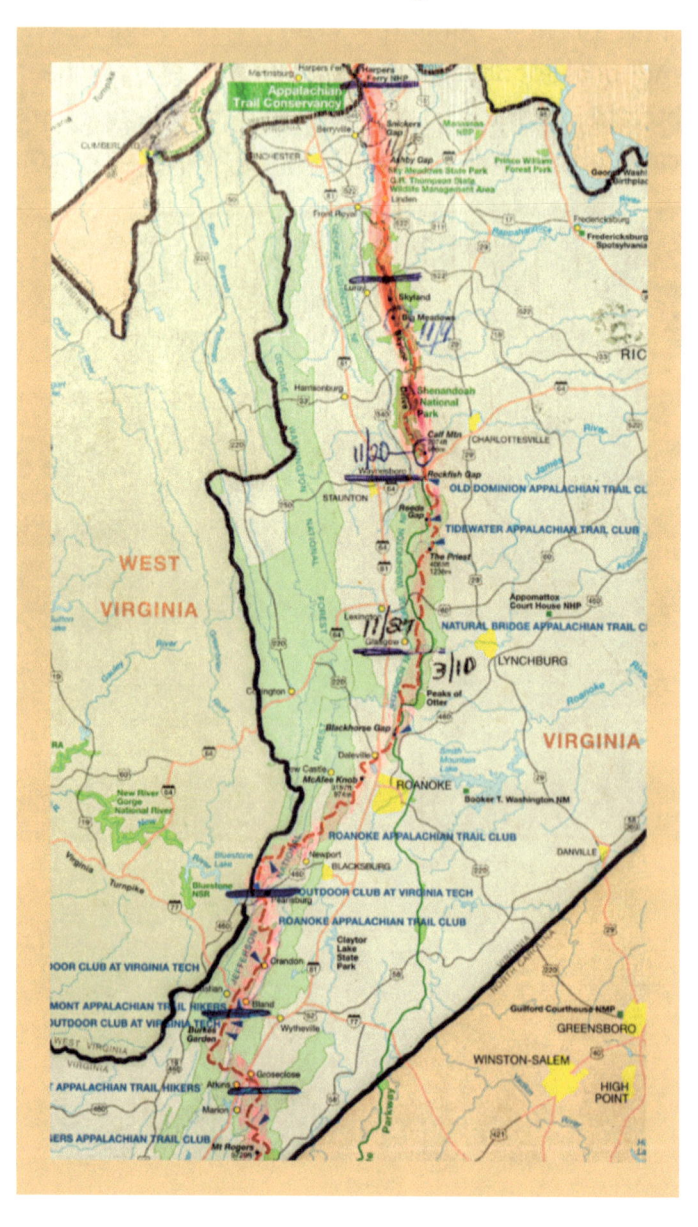

November 1st, 2018

Thru hikers talk about the "Virginia Blues" and I think today I was hit by a triple dose. First, I reluctantly left the only family I had for the previous few months and second, because I now faced over 500 more miles in this state and third, because It was now November and Virginia, although beautiful in the spring and summer, is starting to look a lot like winter. Many hikers find they can't handle the miles, get depressed, and soon quit completely. That didn't bother me as I never let crossing lines get to me. It was fun for sure, but I wasn't consumed by a line. In this moment, I once again felt like I could "smell the hay in the barn". But wait... maybe it wasn't the hay. At that moment a flash of reality hit me and I wondered how can one smell hay 500 miles away.

For now, I'm hiking alone and putting down one foot after another. I enjoyed the solitude and thought about how I could become a better person. The trail in Virginia was easy so far and unlike New England and Pennsylvania, I didn't have to be constantly watching my next step. I would sometimes be so deep in thought and busy "smelling the roses", that I'd miss a blaze or two and have to backtrack to find the trail. Being lost is kind of scary, as the first thing you do is panic. The experts say to stop and relax and think. People that panic usually go further off the trail and get search party lost. It was during one of those moments I decided to invest in a phone app that worked off of satellites, not cell towers, and would show my position and guide me back to the trail. It became indispensable.

I got a text from Thumper saying Fixit had a medical emergency and had to leave the trail. Thumper was with him at the time and was returning to the trail to continue hiking solo. Fixit would rejoin her as soon as he was given the "OK" by the Doctor.

My solo hike was going well as I approached the section known as the "Roller Coaster". It even had a sign welcoming hikers. It was a series of PUDS over ten or twelve short but strenuous climbs with rocky terrain. I kind of enjoyed the change of pace and I soon reached the Sam Moore Shelter. I was alone at first, but then heard the unmistakable sound of kids... Lots of them. It was a Boy Scout troop. They were good, well behaved, and respectful kids and like most kids they were somewhat noisy. Later the scout leader came over to introduce himself and ask a few of the more common questions about thru hiking. The kids commandeered the available picnic table, so I cooked dinner on a rock in front of my shelter. The next morning, I snuck out of the shelter and left the scouts still sleeping.

Around mid-morning, I got a text from Thumper saying she was back on the trail. She was only ten miles behind me and I knew she would catch me soon because she could pour on the speed when she needed it. I told her where my next stop was and she said she'd try to meet up with me.

It was an uneventful and easy hiking day through meadows and pastures. I met and conversed with a few NOBO's that were section hiking and I soon arrived at a blue blazed trail to Dicksdome Shelter. When I got there, it was.... Gone. It had been replaced by the brand new Whiskey Hollow Shelter. How lucky can I get? It had an upper level and a large front porch with plenty of space for cooking and eating. I set up on the second level which is always my choice when it's available.

No sooner did I set up my space when I heard footsteps. It was Thumper and we had a lot of catching up to do. She said Fixit was recovered and was waiting for the doctor to release him. She also filled me in on the late-night reunion in Harpers Ferry as I returned to my room with the party in full swing. I was really happy to see Thumper for a kind of selfish reason. I knew she hiked faster than me and that would push me to make up for some of the ten mile days in Maine and New Hampshire. It worked, the next day we were both flying and knocked off fifteen miles.

Thumper was running low and needed a resupply and I was running low myself, so we decided to hitch into town. They used towns to resupply where I used maildrops. Some of the smaller towns don't have much of a selection and the post office doesn't always deliver either. Sometimes I was in town too early and had to take a zero, and sometimes they just lost my box.

We got a quick ride and found a well-stocked supermarket to resupply. We drew some strange looks, as we found a spot in front of the store to empty our packs and restock our food bags.

We knew the Tom Floyd Shelter was a tough three miles away and that was our destination. But first, we headed to a restaurant for a hot meal. The place had a new owner that was very hiker friendly and had gone to great lengths to attract and serve hikers. She even built locker rooms with what hikers wanted the most... hot showers.

By the time we left, it was getting dark and we still had three more miles to the shelter. I sucked it up, put on my headlamp and just tried to keep Thumper in sight. There were two ascents with a gap in the middle. In the gap there was a strong stream and we headed up the stream to find a place to cross. It seemed like the detour took hours but I'm sure it was only minutes. We found a place to cross and once on the other bank we headed downstream to find the trail. I was really worried and thanked God I was with Thumper, who led the way.

When we arrived at the shelter, we found a young couple already asleep. I set up quietly and Thumper set up her tent outside the shelter. I went to sleep thinking I only had 500 miles to Damascus. Little did I know these last miles would present the biggest test of determination in my lifetime.

I did some serious mileage over the next week. Thumper set the pace and kept me focused and moving as we started leapfrogging and meeting again at camps. I was keeping up with Thumper, but I was having trouble staying ahead of winter. The days were bearable but the nights became colder every day. I recall one night when I caught up with Pony Keg and Blue Dream at a shelter. Another thru hiker showed up with a dog and I thought, maybe a dog would come in handy on a cold night. Sure enough, I was having a hard time staying warm while the guy with the dog had a personal foot warmer.

That same night, a few day hikers showed up at 8:30 pm. It had rained earlier and they were wet and cold. We offered to make space in the shelter, but they declined and set up their tents on the deck outside. They obviously had never heard of hiker midnight, and the laughing, talking, and partying went on. It wasn't long before Pony Keg had enough and gave them a polite but stern lesson in camp courtesy. They were good students, and we were able to get some shuteye. In the morning we tiptoed around their tents and left them sleeping.

I'm glad to be in Virginia where the hiking is easier, and I'll hopefully make up for the slow going in the Northeast. My problem now was going to be the cold. It was staying cold later in the day and I had to add and shed layers to stay warm without sweating.

Rock Spring Hut Shelter,
Photograph taken by Sarah Jones Decker

Next day I rolled into Rock Spring Hut Shelter. I dropped my pack and went to find the water source where I could pump and filter water for the night and the next morning. When I returned to the shelter, I sat to relax and soak in the gorgeous vista. The shelter was set on a long ridge with the open end facing away from the mountain. The view looked like it was cleared but looking closer, there were no stumps so it must have been natural.

I noticed a cabin a couple hundred yards down the mountain and decided to go check it out. It was oriented the same way as the shelter with a view through the trees. As I walked around to the front, there sat Pony Keg and Thumper having a Safety Meeting. These meetings were common on the trail with young and some older hikers. It involved a usually home rolled cannabis filled wrap that relaxed the participant and seemed to make them happier and most times hungrier. They invited me as they always did and I again declined. It was times like these when I wished I would've packed a cold Heineken. On my way up to the shelter, I passed a couple guys headed down to the cabin. I guessed they had rented the cabin.

The wind was picking up and the temperature was dropping as the sun went down. I set my tent up in the shelter even though it was a breach of shelter etiquette. I would have moved it back out if anyone else showed up, but no one did. As I ate dinner, I could hear more people coming and they sounded like a party was already starting. Two more guys passed the shelter and headed to the cabin. No hello, no wave, no nod, no nothing.

What was to follow would be the worst night I endured for the entire 2,200 miles. The party in the cabin got louder and more intense. It reached a point I began to worry someone might get hurt. I was afraid to look at my watch, but it seemed to go on all night. They finally either passed out or went to sleep, but I was so keyed up I couldn't sleep. To make matters worse, I began hearing rustling noises outside my tent. I looked out and couldn't see a thing in the dark. My imagination ran wild and I pictured everything from a mouse to a black bear. Before I could sleep, the sun began to rise.

It was very cold, and my hypothermia fears returned. I crawled out of my tent and put on every piece of clothes I had and then just sat there staring. What happened next is embarrassing but true. While I sat staring into space, I heard the same sound that kept me from sleeping. It wasn't a mouse or a bear, but a flap on my rainfly blowing in the wind.

I could see where one of the partyers from last night had pitched his tent nearby. I also remembered one of them was talking on a cell phone. I could see someone stirring in the tent, so I went over and told him I was in bad shape and could I use his phone to get a pickup at the closest road. He said "sure, as soon as I pack up my things". I thanked him and told him I was going back to my tent to get in my sleeping bag to try and warm up. Next thing I know the partyer's all left. So much for my phone call.

I climbed out of the sleeping bag again and watched Thumper and Pony Keg walking up the trail. I mentioned the cold and Thumper said, "You need to get moving". She was right. I was emotionally depressed and physically drained of energy. I thought if I could get some food in me, I might be able to jump start my metabolism and stop the shivering.

Before I could light my stove, three young guys walked up and we greeted each other. One of them said "Sir, are you okay?" I said, "Not really, I think I'm hypothermic." All three Angels jumped into action. One went to my tent, removed my sleeping bag and after unzipping it, wrapped it around me like a blanket. The second one took two chemical hand warmers out of his pack and gave them to me to get my hands working again. And the third young man took out his phone and called a Ranger, who literally arrived in minutes as he was able to take a forest road to within 250 feet of the shelter. He asked if I could walk to his truck and I said, "I think so". I gave each of the guys a hug and thanked them for their help. Their timing couldn't have been better for me. All I could think of now, was that maybe I should have attended the Safety Meeting last night.

Once inside the heated vehicle, my condition improved but I still couldn't stop trembling. It took another fifteen or twenty minutes to stop shaking. The ranger said he wasn't supposed to take me out of the park, but he said he was going to make an exception and bring me into Elkton to a hiker friendly hotel he knew of. I told him that would be great. For some reason I asked him if he thought I could continue my hike if I found an outfitter and purchased some cold weather gear. He just said, "I don't see why not". Maybe he thought I was thinking of quitting, but I wasn't.

He dropped me off and I thanked him profusely. I had a hot chocolate in the lobby of the hotel and when I reached the room, I cranked up the heat and jumped into a hot shower, a longer than usual hot shower.

The next day I took a zero and headed into town to find an outfitter. When there, a guy was very helpful and set me up with everything I'd need to survive the cold. I found out a woman that worked at the hotel had a son who was an Uber driver which would make it easier going to town or back to the trail.

The next morning had an ugly start. A fog rolled in and it started to rain, but I knew I had to suck it up and get going. The day was a harbinger of things to come and the shelter that evening was a long walk down two side trails. The cold day got even colder that night but my new gear did its job and I stayed relatively warm. I was the only person in the shelter that night and I slept well. I woke to a frozen landscape the next morning. I had remembered to take my water into the sleeping bag and that worked to keep it from freezing.

On the trail again, I was having a good day until I came to the entrance to the skyline drive. I was met by two Park Rangers in a truck that advised me to get off the trail. They said some severe weather was forecast for the next day, and here I thought it already was severe. Since the closest town was still Elkton, I called the Uber driver and he picked me up. Back to the hotel and a junk food dinner followed by my new bad habit... Ice Cream.

That night the power in the hotel went out, but I didn't realize it until dawn when I woke up. I opened the front door and noticed there was ice everywhere. No snow, just ice. It wasn't the kind of scene one wakes up to in Fort Lauderdale, but then again, I'm in Northern Virginia in mid-November. When I went to the front desk, the woman said it was the worst storm they've had in fifteen years. She said it might be a while as power lines were down all over. She was kind enough to ask me if I needed anything, like blankets. The power wasn't restored until the next day. I started calling the

Shenandoah National Park (SNP) and the message was not encouraging. They said the Skyline Drive and the Park were both closed, due to the ice storm.

It occurred to me that the trail basically follows the Skyline Drive highway and crosses over it some thirty times. So, I'm thinking why not hike the road until the trail is clear enough. There were downed trees on both, but the highway had better footing, and more room to navigate around the fallen trees. It was only a forty-five mile section and I hoped it would get me past the area affected by the storm.

I called the Appalachian Trail Conference and they assured me it was permissible, for safety reasons, to road walk or even skip a section if the trail became impassable. Next, I called the SNP ranger station to see if was legal to walk the road to avoid the closed section of trail and they said, "At your own risk". Alrighty then... I'm outta here in the morning.

I got to the entrance to the Skyline Drive bright and early. It was only a few hundred feet to the trailhead and when I got there, I had a clear view downhill. Quite a bit of the trail was visible and in that short section I could see half a dozen large trees down across the path.

As I stood there gazing at the power of Mother Nature, I was reminded of a hike several years ago with Bob, Carmen and her son Angel. ***We were on a multi-day hike in the Smokies when a freak storm came out of nowhere and nearly blew us out of the woods. It's funny how these storms almost always hit at night. Living in Florida, we've experienced hurricane winds almost every summer but we didn't expect to be hit by one in the North Carolina mountains. It raged all night while we laid in our tents wondering if the trees would*** *fall on us, or if the creek would overflow from the rains, or how many days it would take to notify our families. The newspaper a few day later said the winds were clocked at 100 plus mph, and several people were injured from trees falling on campers and motor homes in Cades Cove and other parts of the park.*

Forty-five mile road walk on Skyline Drive after the ice storm

Back in Virginia, this was a no brainer, and up the road I hiked. It started out okay, but the further I went it became obvious that the trees were down on the road and the trail. Over, under, and around I went. Sometimes on my belly (or what was left of it) and other times fighting limbs, trunks, and craters where large trees once stood. Other times I'd have to get off the road to find a way around a downed tree. After falling on black ice on the road, I took to walking on the road shoulder whenever possible.

After about fifteen miles, I came upon a wayside. I think it was called Loft Mountain. These waysides are like a service plaza without gasoline. They have a restaurant and a gift shop, but on this day, they were closed up tight. I decided this would be my home for the night. The place had been winterized so the water was shut off, but I drank little today, so I had enough to get me through the night and started the next day. There was a big parking lot that had a sectioned off space with picnic tables in it. I arranged the tables in a square and set up my tent using the table legs to tie off my tent. The trash cans were bear proof and empty, so I put my food bag in one of them. That night I got the best sleep I'd get on the trail.

By the next day, the black ice disappeared, the ascents became more gradual, and the overlooks were more grandiose than ever. It was getting later in November, but bright fall colors still covered the mountains. The miles clicked by and I was getting tired, but I was determined to reach Rockfish Gap in ten miles.

I had an adrenaline rush when after 1,800 miles of trail, I finally saw a bear. This was a small cub and I knew Mama was nearby. I didn't want to get between the cub and the mama, so I kept scanning the woods for her. It was walking down the center of the road toward me so I stopped, but the bear kept coming. I then made a deliberate move to the high side of the road and it finally went down the mountain. I kept checking for mama bear but I didn't see her so I got my nerve back and marched on.

Beautiful fall colors

A half hour later, I had an instant replay. This time the bear was full grown. I didn't bother to check its gender and I think it was too far from the cub to be the cub's mama. This bear bolted down the mountain when it spotted me.

My legs felt like cement, but I knew Rockfish Gap and the town of Waynesboro were within reach. About three miles out, I came upon a road crew clearing storm debris from the road. I told them I just walked forty-two miles in the last two days and they asked me for a damage assessment, which I happily shared. I found out they were A.T.C. volunteers. I thanked them and moved on to keep my legs working. About a mile and a half down the road they passed me as they headed to town. I thought they might offer me a ride, but they didn't. At first, I was disappointed, but then I thought about it and being an AT purist, I wouldn't be able to look at myself in a mirror if I cheated even a mile and a half.

When I reached the toll plaza at Rockfish Gap, I felt like I'd just run a Marathon. Actually, I just walked a marathon and added 3.8 miles to that, making it a thirty mile day. I was tired and quickly called Lyft for a ride. After a few cold minutes, the driver called and wanted to know where I was. I told him and he said he was half a mile down the road and couldn't drive any further. I asked him to please wait, and I hurried down the closed road to meet him.

Man, that nice warm car felt good. He dropped me off at a Days Inn in Waynesboro. All I wanted was a hot shower, a hot meal, and a warm, comfortable bed in that order. I would worry about tomorrow, tomorrow.

Well, tomorrow is here and now I was worried. I had no idea what the trail looked like ahead. The forty-five miles in two days took a toll on my legs and I could barely move them. I figured I earned a zero so I had the hotel's continental breakfast and headed to a Walmart a mile down the road to resupply.

Now I'm getting lonely... It's Thanksgiving, a day my family always got together at my mom's house. I walked to a nearby Cracker Barrel but the line came out their front door and down the porch. I found a small restaurant and it was almost empty. I had dinner and between the food and the service I knew why they had no lines.

I headed back to my room to ponder my fate as I was running out of options. Rockfish Gap is where the Skyline Drive turns into the Blue Ridge Parkway. The trail doesn't follow the BRP the way the SLD did so road walking wasn't a viable option. That left me with three choices:

1. Push on and hope the trail is passable.

2. Try to skip the storm damage.

3. Bail and come back in the spring.

I chose the first option and hit the trail early in the morning. It wasn't bad first thing but conditions quickly deteriorated. It became as impassable as it could get and I took all day, just to get five miles to the Paul C. Wolfe Shelter. I lost the trail three times because it was obliterated by the storm and falling trees. One big tree forced me to crawl under it and my pack straps tangled with a branch. I had to crawl out of my pack, then go back to retrieve it. Option one wasn't working out well. My only hope was that the five mile days would be short lived.

The shelter was one of the nicer ones with an upper deck, so I staked out my usual spot. There was a small creek near the shelter where I could take care of water needs. I didn't expect any company as there aren't that many people (like me) crazy enough to be out in this weather. It was dark when I crawled into my sleeping bag, when I saw three women, college age or a little older. We introduced ourselves and I asked them how they were ever able to find this place in the dark. One said they had a late start from Rockfish Gap and frankly, they didn't know how they did it either.

They discussed going back to Rockfish Gap in the morning. One of them seemed to be more experienced than the other two and she suggested they bushwhack up the mountain to where it crosses the Blue Ridge Parkway, and roadwalk back. I wasn't asked my opinion, so none was offered. But If they had asked, I would've told them, "No way".

It rained hard all night and I heard the girls talking, and packing up, so I got up to say goodbye. Much to my surprise they left the shelter and headed straight up the mountain. They were slipping and sliding up the muddy mountain side and hugging trees as they went. They were wearing blue jeans which probably didn't help. I said a little prayer that they made it okay and fixed myself some hot coffee and oatmeal. I walked down to the creek to see where the trail picked up on the other side. I found it but I also found a new dilemma. The rain from the night before had swelled the creek to twice it's size. I walked a quarter mile looking for a place to cross. I considered fording but the creek was running way too fast, and my recent bouts with hypothermia forced me to look at more conservative options. I didn't want to backtrack, but that's what I had to do. It was five miles back to Rockfish Gap, and it looked like another wasted day.

When I made it back, I guess I was depressed as I couldn't think clearly. All I could think about was that my hike may be over. I was in desperate need of some moral support and my beautiful wife Carmen and my old friend Bob stepped up to the challenge. Carmen reminded me of how stubborn and determined I was and then said in perfect English, "You aren't going to quit now!". Bob, always the lighthearted jokester, lifted my spirits. He jumped into action and from his home in Sebring, Florida. He started making calls. In the *AT Guide* by David Miller, he found a hostel in the town of Glasgow that offered shuttle service. The town was over thirty miles south of Waynesboro and they could slack pack me back north... Sign me up. The shuttle driver was a thru hiker himself that had run out of money and took the driver job, so he could eventually get back on his feet and the trail.

He was kind enough to take me to the town of Buena Vista where Carmen had sent a maildrop to the post office. The box contained new boots that would be my last pair. I was averaging 450 to 550 miles on my boots. The hostel was a two-bedroom home with two sets of bunkbeds in each bedroom. My shuttle driver "Frog" was also the caretaker of the hostel. He gave me a thirty second tour of the town as it consisted of a general store and a small restaurant.

I checked in to the hostel and staked out a spot in one if the bedrooms. I then went to the general store and bought some items for dinner and the next morning's breakfast. We had kitchen privileges in the hostel. Later, a southbound hiker checked in. He didn't say much and kept to himself. I didn't even get his name. We dropped him off at the trailhead road crossing and then went thirty miles south where Frog dropped me off. I made several calls to the ATC to report the condition of the trails and they were very helpful, giving me information that they had on the trail ahead of me.

This slack pack section would be my first since Maine, when I only carried my tent and two days of food. Things went well considering this was the most strenuous hiking I'd found in Virginia. I had one climb left and it was Apple Orchard Mountain, a 4,000-footer. There were only a handful this high in the entire state.

As I began the ascent, I knew I was only a couple miles from Thunder Hill Shelter, my home for the night. The wind picked up and the temperature started to drop. I looked for a "facilatree" to block the wind while I relieved myself and I thought I'd get frostbite before I could get my gloves on. I was dreaming that this shelter would have windows, a door, and a heater. But I wasn't going to bet on it. I passed an FAA station and antenna, complete with chain link fences, standing in sharp contrast to its surroundings. There was a clearing for the FAA station, and it was there I met the southbound hiker we dropped off that morning. There were no trees to block the cold wind, so we just exchanged a quick fist bump and raced (me north and him south) for the tree line and the cover it provided.

As I started to descend, I saw another big wind blocking tree and ducked behind it to tie my new boots. I seemed to be having a problem with them loosening up as I walked. I was motoring along a well graded gradual downhill section and feeling really good because it looked like there was little storm damage here.

Maybe I spoke too soon... I came upon a relatively small tree across the trail that could easily be stepped over. As I did, my foot planted on a branch that was on the ground. My foot felt stable, but when I brought my trailing leg over the trunk of the tree, I heard a loud *SNAP*! I knew right away the *snap* wasn't the branch, but it was my ankle. My foot had slipped off the branch and rolled my ankle to the outside. I've rolled my ankle before and at first this didn't seem that different, but when I tried to put weight on my foot, I knew this wasn't just a rolled ankle. As I hopped on one foot waiting for the pain to subside, I looked down and my foot was dangling there, limp. I tried to move my foot and there was no response. I couldn't put any weight on the foot, so I knew my long-term plans were about to change. Then it occurred to me that I better start worrying, or working, on a short-term plan. I thought many times during my planning stage of this hike about what I'd do if this moment happened. First, I thought, "don't panic, stay calm".

I didn't consider staying where I was because they would find me frozen if I stayed put. In my mind I figured my only option was to keep moving. I tried using my trekking pole as a crutch, but every step was agony. Every time any weight was put on the ankle, I would scream. I think I was hoping someone, somewhere would hear me and come save me. I passed a section called the Guillotine. It was named after its odd rock formations and I considered hunkering down for the night in some cave like rocks that would get me out of the wind. I pushed that bad idea aside and decided to make the shelter, only half a mile away. If I could get there by hopping, sliding, crawling, and using trees to pull me, it might just work.

I was now barely inching along. After a quarter mile of struggling, I had a surprise. Instead of reaching the shelter, I reached the Blue Ridge Parkway first. Pain had my mind confused and wandering and I had forgotten that the trail crossed the BRP. I was going to get to the shelter, try to stay warm, and try to make it out and call for help in the morning. But that plan changed in a hurry.

I took out my phone to see if I had service and I did. It took several calls to get through to 911 but the call finally went through, and the 911 operator was a great help. I gave her my location and she assured me they would be on their way. It was very cold and I wasn't moving, so I tried to hop, move my arms, and the leg that was still able to move to stay warm. After an hour, I began to worry about hypothermia again. I began looking for a spot to pitch my tent if they didn't show, when I saw flashing red lights coming up the road.

Tears welled up in my eyes when I saw the first responders. They apologized for the long wait but they said a section of the road was closed due to the ice storm and they had to call to get keys to open a gate. I was just happy they were there and I was overcome with gratitude and appreciation. During the ride to the hospital, they told me the 911 operator said I was on the trail and they may have to carry me who knows how far out of the woods. They said when they saw me on the side of the road, they were so happy, they began cheering and high fiving. There was no doubt my mother stood with me the whole time, helping through another bump in the road of life like she always did. I love you mom...

It was a slow day in the emergency room, and they were on me from three sides. I was wheeled to have x-rays and they gave me something for the pain. The doctor came in and said he had good news and bad news. "The bad news is you have a broken ankle, and the good news is, its spiral fracture and won't require surgery, screws, and plates". They would put me into a temporary cast that would get me back to Fort Lauderdale where they recommended, I see an orthopedic specialist as soon as possible.

It was now time to call Carmen (Brown Eyes) and deliver the news. She knew how bummed I was and how much effort I put in, so there was no more trying to talk me out of it. She said she'd check on return flights and call me back. I called

Frog at the last hostel, and he said he'd pick me up at the hospital. I was waiting for Frog when Carmen called me back to say my sister Anne Marie and her husband Larry would drive up to pick me up and take me home to Fort Lauderdale.

I felt my dream of thru hiking the AT was over as Frog picked me up at the hospital and we drove back to the hostel. It was a quiet ride back to Glasgow. We stopped at a restaurant for dinner and returned to the hostel. For the foreseeable future I would be taping plastic bags around my lower leg and trying to sleep in a recliner. I hated the uncertainty about how long I might be laid up or if I'd be able to return to the trail within the one year thru hike limit. My spirits were up because I knew Anne Marie was on her way to get me back home. When they arrived a couple nights later, they brought a special surprise, and it had brown eyes. I heard the car pull up to the hostel and I knew it was my sister and her husband Larry. They knocked on the door and Frog answered. I heard a loud, "Where's Healy" and knew Carmen came with them. It was totally unexpected, and since it was late November, it wasn't too early for a Christmas present.

Chapter Fifteen

Fort Lauderdale & Central Virginia

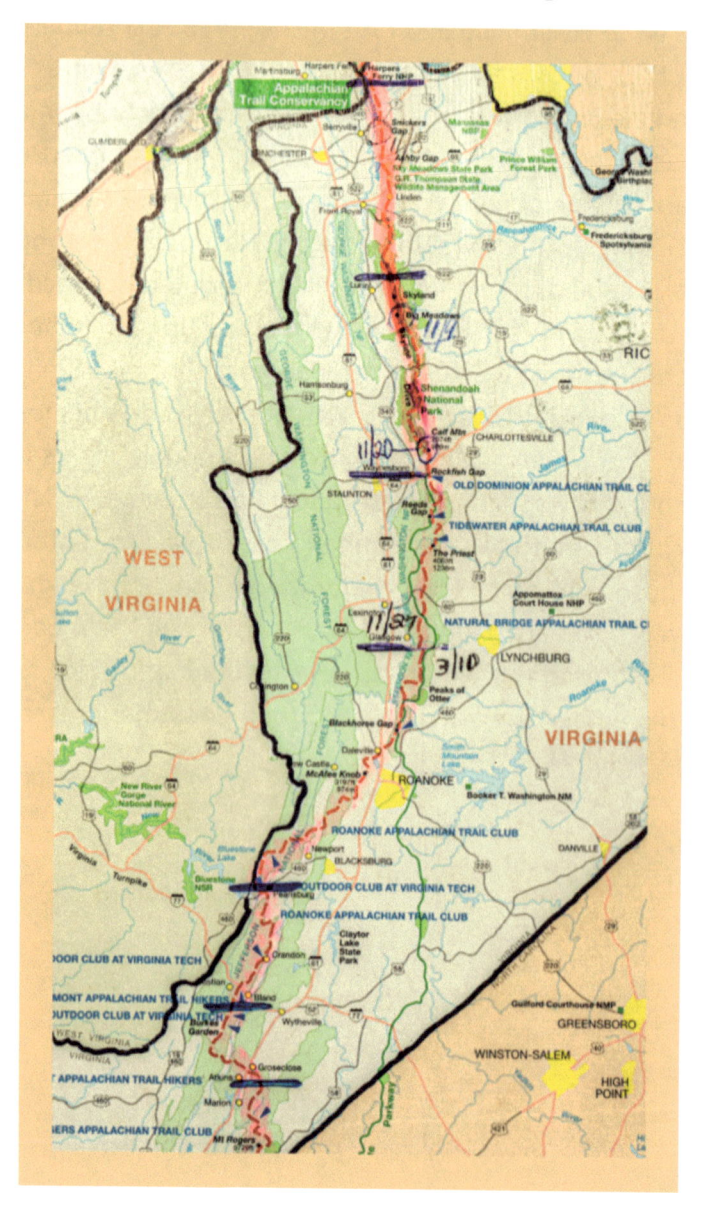

The ride back to Fort Lauderdale was a long one. I was now with my family, but I couldn't help but think about the 288 miles that I needed to complete the thru hike. To be truly considered a thru hike it has to be completed in a twelve-month period. I was eager to get home and find a doctor to see if I had the time to recover enough to return to Virginia. I had no interest in starting over or completing the hike outside the twelve-month window. Carmen and others had done enough already to support the hike and to make my dream come true. Through the hike, I raised over $7,500 for The American Cancer Society, mostly with small donations and with help from my friends, and many people that I didn't know, but had heard of my plans to hike. The money was raised by Crowd Rise, and they take a little off the top. All the rest goes to the Cancer Society. I wanted to do what I could to honor my son and my sister that both passed away recently from the disease.

Brian, a good friend of mine, hooked me up with a friend and client of his that was a non-surgical orthopedic specialist. I made an appointment and when he looked at the x-rays and my ankle, he said, "Brian told me about you, so let's see what we can do to get you back on the trail to finish within the time limits." "Maybe I'm not cooked after all", I thought. I felt like the old fire in my belly had been reignited and I was raring to get to work on rehab. Well, not really as that would all take time and I needed to take it slow. I made up my mind to do exactly what Dr. Jack Trainor had ordered. I wasn't going to rush my recovery, because I really trusted him when he said he could get me back to Virginia to finish.

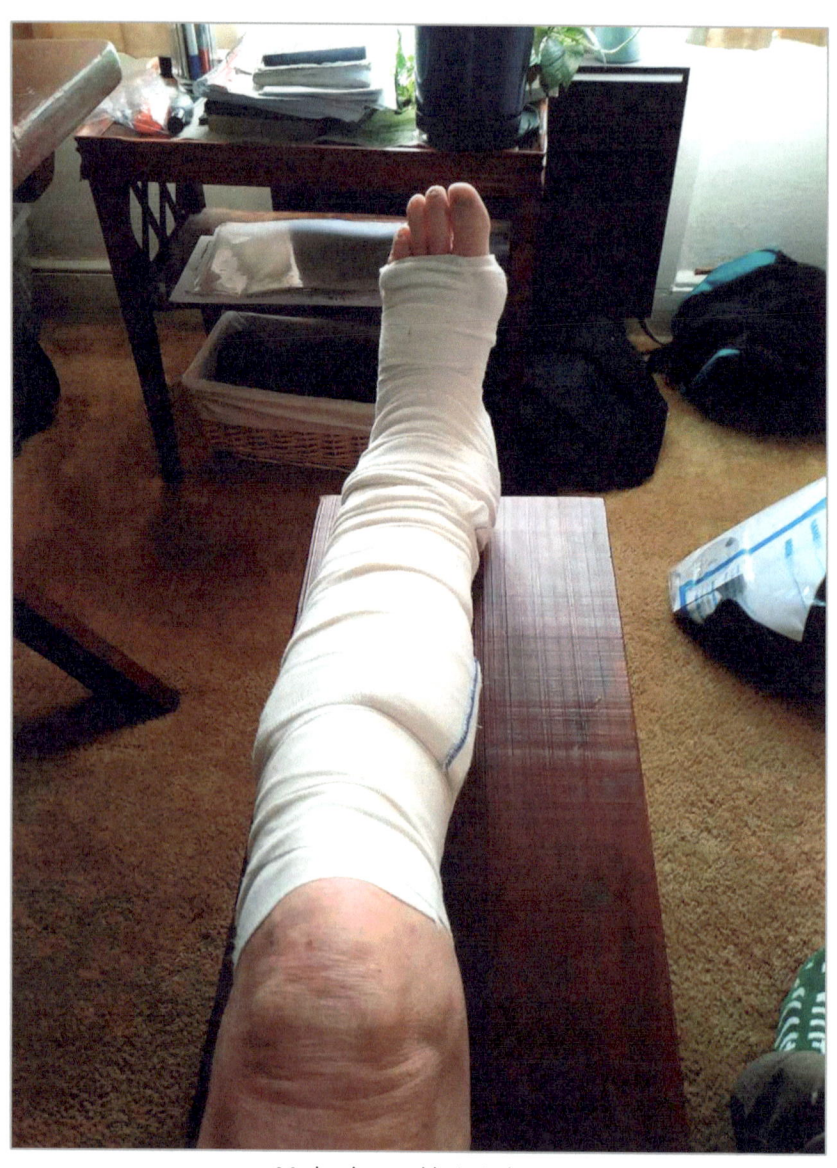

My broken ankle in its' cast

His first direction was: No weight on the ankle and foot for the next six weeks. I've never been a very patient person, so this wouldn't be easy. The six weeks seemed like an eternity. Carmen got me a scooter contraption that my knee rested on and my foot trailed behind me hanging in air and keeping pressure off my ankle. Stage two was physical therapy. I had physical therapy for my knee years before, and it was more like torture. This was more like a workout and included exercises to improve my balance. I thought maybe it would improve my dancing, but I guess I just need more rhythm.

My simulated short hikes around the Fort Lauderdale airport, wearing my pack with bottles filled with water helped me get back on track, and in March 2019, I felt ready for the trail. Dr. Jack and his remarkable staff had pulled it off. My leg is now ready to climb a mountain and I hope the rest of me is ready too. Carmen's good cooking and the ice cream habit I carried home have added a few pounds, but my rehab hikes, the PT, and the patience paid off. Like they say on the trail, "If you're not in shape when you get to the trail, keep walking and you will be". I'm ready for my biggest test yet, as I board a plane heading to Roanoke, Virginia.

It's March 2019 and this is my last chance. I'll have just over three weeks to complete the 288 miles and pick up my completion certificate. I'll need to average around 13 miles a day including zero days. While I was off the trail, I communicated with Frog through email. He was back on the trail himself, so I called the Glasgow hostel and arranged a pickup at the Roanoke airport. I soon met my driver, put my gear in his car, and we headed to the hostel. We had a long ride, so we had a nice conversation about how he grew up in the small town of Glasgow.

I was like a racehorse at the gate, chomping at the bit to take that first big step. But then it was back to reality. It snowed overnight and was still snowing when I woke up. I had zero experience winter hiking, except my not so pleasant walk in ice-covered Virginia last November. I worried the snow covering the trail would cause me to lose the trail and slow me down to where a thirteen mile day would be impossible. I decided to delay my start by one day, and I called Carmen so she wouldn't worry.

My ride was there early the next morning. My driver wasn't sure where the trailhead was on Jennings Creek where I exited the trail last November but I told him I was pretty sure I'd recognize it. I was wrong and we passed it. He drove back and we saw the trailhead, unloaded my gear, and I was finally, after almost three and a half months, back on the trail.

I must have been on an adrenaline rush all day. I started with a decent climb up Cove Mountain, followed by ten PUD's. My loss of conditioning was becoming painfully apparent, but I caught a break when the trail crossed the Blue Ridge Parkway several times and the elevation stayed mostly level. The trail stayed level and I walked into the Wilson Creek Shelter after a sixteen mile day. As I approached, I heard voices from the shelter and I feared it was full, but it was only a young couple talking.

He was a former AT thru hiker, and they parked their car on the Blue Ridge Parkway and took the AT crossing down to this shelter. They had a big birthday party planned for a little girl. This happened earlier in my hike in Pennsylvania when I was with Troop Leader. Shelters near the highway are usually very busy with people celebrating a special day or just out for a picnic. We had a nice conversation and they said they would be gone before dark, and be sure to clean up after themselves. Friends and family began to arrive and the party soon began. We had a great time and they shared with me like I was one of the family. As promised, they left before dark and they cleaned up and left no trace. I then sat in my empty shelter.

The next day was more easy terrain and I pushed out a twenty mile day. I went through and around a lot of meadows and fields. Some were fenced and stiles were becoming common. They were put there to keep live stock in and usually were steps over a fence or wire and other times there was a maze that apparently confused me and the livestock.

I had a "major goose bumps" moment when I rolled into Daleville. *Several years before, Carmen and I were on a multiday backpack trip with two of her five brothers. We were northbound and we had to climb the Dragons Tooth, Mcafee Knob, and Tinker Cliffs (Virginia's Triple Crown). We had a good time but I had another hypothermia scare. I forget what month it was, but we had just passed Mcafee Knob when an early season snow fell and we ended up at a shelter where I was cold and wet and began shivering uncontrollably. Thank god for Carmen as she set up our tent in the shelter and climbed into my sleeping bag and warmed me with body heat. I wished she was here now in Virginia, but it's not that cold and she's back in Florida.*

We ended that hike in Daleville and, to maintain an old hiking tradition we had, looked for a diner or restaurant where we could have a "pig out", which is what we called our after-hike gorging or sometimes called a "feeding frenzy". When at the chosen spot we would always apologize to the waitress for anything we might say or do. That usually made her very nervous and she'd pay close attention to our needs.

Back to Virginia in 2019... I was in a convenience store parking lot, so I took a break to shamelessly stuff myself with some junk food. A honey bun and a big bag of Fritos should do the trick. Now back into the woods and headed the nine miles to the Lamberts Meadow Shelter. I made it with ease, after another twenty mile day. There was a meadow and a creek near the shelter and a young couple sitting in the shelter. They were very young as in teenagers and when I arrived, they moved down by the creek and set up their tent. They both jumped into the creek for a swim, then dried off and jumped into their tent. I guess they needed privacy... I heard some giggling, but never saw them again.

Another hiker walked in, but hardly said a word. He just set up his hammock and kept to himself. It looks like I'd have an empty shelter again... Yay!

I got a great night's sleep and was up and on the trail by 6:00 am. My first challenge of the day was going to be the Virginia Triple Crown. I knew the climb would be strenuous, but I was up for it. I was looking forward to the views at the summit, as the last time here there was heavy fog. This time it was cold but clear. I paused at Mcafee Knob and saw the shelter where Carmen had saved me from Hypothermia. The views on this day from Mcafee Knob were stupendous. It's supposedly the most photographed view on the AT and I couldn't resist asking a tourist to take my picture. My plan was to do fifteen miles today to the Four Pines hostel, but I tweaked something in my knee on the descent from Mcafee. When I came to a road crossing five miles short of the hostel, I called Joe, the owner and asked for a pickup.

It was an interesting hostel. It was a very large converted garage. At one end was about eight bunks, then a common area with chairs, a sofa, and a table. On one wall was a sink, a small refrigerator, and a bathroom. Joe and a friend were making sausage and as I watched, he said there was a convenience store down the road and I could use his truck. He said the keys were in it and there was a jar between the seats for gas money. I ended up with the place to myself, as it was too early for either north or south bounders in Virginia.

In the morning my knee felt better but to be sure, I'd slack pack the five miles I missed the day before. Joe's wife drove me to where I left off and I was flying so fast I thought I might beat her back to the hostel. The knee was okay, so I started for the challenging climb up the last of the triple crown, The Dragon's Tooth. It was damp and overcast when I left the hostel the second time. I could see it was a very steep and rocky ascent at times. It reminded me of the Whites of New Hampshire where rebars were drilled into the rocks to help with footholds. The good news for me was that it wasn't a very long climb. I made it unscathed, but not unafraid.

Next, was a very long ridge walk. It was slow, but the weather was improving and I finally saw a couple NOBO thru hikers, that probably left Springer Mountain in Georgia in early March. I would have asked except they blew by me so fast they almost knocked me off the trail. I guess they were in a hurry.

For the next few days, I hiked alone with a rare passing hiker. This section would be the perfect version of the perfect hike, seen through a non-hiker's eyes. There was a little bit of everything, from 4,000 foot climbs to valleys, creeks, pastures, fields, and farmhouses. It was topped off with mountain air, views, and sunshine.

I must admit, some of these climbs shouldn't have been so difficult. During my three-and-a-half-month layoff, I had lost my trail legs and now had to find them again. My rebuilt, better than ever, ankle felt great thanks to my rehab team back in Fort Lauderdale.

As I was closing in on Pearisburg, I passed an elderly female day hiker and asked her how far the next road crossing was. Good news, she said it was about a mile. Word on the trail was that a great hostel was in the town. It was called, Angels Rest Hikers' Haven. When I reached the road my phone said, "no service". This happened way too often and it bothered me when I saw others make calls while my phone sat there.

I knew it was miles into town and I wanted a shuttle, so I started walking and looking for someone with a phone. I saw two teenage girls come out of a house and go to a car, so I asked if they could help. They went back to the house and came out with their mother and a phone. I called the hostel and they said they would pick me up in an hour. I waited in the sun on the road for the shuttle. It was cold but he soon rolled up and I jumped into the toasty, heated car.

The hostel had an interesting set up. It was operated by three young guys, all former thru hikers, that shared the chores. It was a pretty big property and the lady that owned it had a house on site, but I never saw her. There was a big open area for tenters, with a firepit, a bunkhouse with a laundry room, and a mobile home that had an office and two private rooms.

As I registered, I noticed a flyer that advertised a multi-day slack pack challenge. All you had to do was hike sixty-five miles in four days and you'd be rewarded with a nice embroidered patch for your effort. The hostel would provide the shuttle and the day pack. I was intrigued by the challenge, so I signed up. With about 150 miles left I was now a man on a mission. I opted for one of the private rooms in the trailer. It was only ten bucks more than the bunkhouse and I would sleep better. There was a supermarket and a Mexican restaurant about a mile away on a paved road, but the hostel had a very short trail through a wooded area that took you to the back of the shopping center... Good thinking.

I took off the next morning from the same spot that they had picked me up the day before. I crossed a road, carefully stepped across a cow pasture, and began a gradual ascent. I had extra layers of clothes as the temperatures were in the mid-thirties. I began to sweat after a few miles, so I found a fence post to hang the day pack and began removing layers. I put on the little day pack and headed up the hill.

After another hour or more, I suddenly got a strange feeling. Something felt different about the grip on my trekking poles. I took off my gloves and my heart hit the floor, as I realized my wedding ring was gone. Almost immediately, I knew the what and why... The night before I noticed a blister on my ring finger. I was concerned about swelling and infection, so I soaped up the finger and took the ring off. I first thought of putting it in my pack, but decided it would be too easy to lose, so I put it on my pinky finger where it was loose but seemed to stay. That was a bad idea. When I stopped to shed a layer, I took my gloves off and the ring must have gone flying out. My little pinky apparently had some serious shrinkage. I was thinking I should make a list of the things I lost on this hike, but then I realized the things I didn't lose would be a shorter list.

    I thought about going back to look, but the two or three hours missed would mean I'd miss my shuttle, so I decided to come back another day or take a zero to come back to look for the ring. When the shuttle driver pulled up later, he asked how my day went. I gave him the good news, then the bad news and all he could say was, "Man that sucks".

    I had great weather for the next couple days and earned my vortex patch, from Hikers Haven. I was looking forward to the patch I earned. Back at the hostel, I told the driver I was heading to the Mexican restaurant for dinner. I had a mini pig out to celebrate my miles and the fact that I was knocking on the Damascus front door.

    When I returned to the hostel, all three guys that ran the place were standing by the mobile home waiting for me. I thought they were taking a break, when one of them said, "Congratulations TAR, you earned your patch, but we gave you something extra". He then handed it to me. I was so excited to get the patch, I really didn't look that close at it. One of them said, "Look a little closer", and when I did, I saw the patch was rolled up and pushed into my wedding band. I couldn't contain my emotions and I started tearing up, jumping up and down, and hugging all three of them. The shuttle driver that picked me up the day I lost the ring had listened to me and was familiar with the spot I described. Without me knowing, the shuttle driver returned to where I told him the ring was lost. He found the post where I took off my gloves and hung the day pack, looked down, and there, sitting on some leaves, was my ring… Talk about a miracle.

The next day was to be my last slack pack day. The guys at the hostel said they would take my full pack ahead to Woods Hole hostel, a one-day hike ahead. I would leave the day pack there and continue on. I got there around noon but no one was there. I peeked into a window and I could see my pack sitting in a corner, so I sat down and waited. It was a picturesque and quaint place. In 1986 the Woods' discovered and bought this chestnut log cabin that was built in the 1880's. They revitalized the place, built a real nice bunkhouse, and added cows and sheep. The legacy was continued by the granddaughter, Neville, and her husband, with an emphasis on sustainable living, bee keeping, farming, gardening, pottery, and yoga. Heating was from wood stoves and woodburning furnaces.

While I waited, I occupied my time by exploring the property. When Neville arrived, she checked me in and said she offered communal meals and slack packing options. Say no more! Slack packing was turning into a great way to build up miles in a shorter period of time. She didn't have any day packs, so I will use the one I wore there and return it to Hiker Haven later.

For the next several days, I became a NOBO again. Neville and I worked out a plan where she would shuttle me forty miles south to an AT trail head, and I would start hiking back toward the hostel as far as I could go, then I'd call her to shuttle me back. I'd repeat this until the last day, when the next morning she'd bring me to the trailhead I started on the first day, and I would be a SOBO again.

Everything went like clockwork, except for my GPS app. That seemed to be confused by me changing directions. It would show me approaching a road crossing when I was really going the other way. I'm sure it had to be a user error. I just relied on my instinct like I did before I had the app.

My next planned stop was a hostel near the town of Bland. The problem was the hostel was about twelve miles from the trailhead. Neville came through again. She remembered a guy that had a shuttle service in that area and called him. Luckily, he was available and agreed to meet me at the trail head. The next morning, I had a great breakfast prepared by Neville. We were joined by a middle-aged couple that were doing a section hike. They wanted to hear all about my hike and kept telling me how impressed the were by what I had done. I was humbled, and for the next few hours my hat wouldn't fit my head.

The drive back to Virginia 615, the point south of Woods Hole where I started my slack pack, was a long one and I had a seventeen-mile hike, but we were on the road early so it was doable. The day went well, and I reached the road to meet my shuttle at 4:00 pm. The road looked to be in the middle of nowhere and wasn't marked. I could have easily missed it. The shuttle was already there and he said he didn't wait too long.

As we left the trail head, he informed me he didn't take plastic. It was cash only. That was the first time that happened in 2,000 miles. When I was preparing for this hike, I read where you should always carry some cash for situations like this. I checked my backpacker's wallet (a plastic baggie) and found I still came up short. We had to turn around and go to a convenience store where I tried to use a credit card, but I'd never set up a pin number for it. After three phone calls and twenty minutes, I got the pin and the cash. The shuttle guy was patient, and I was glad I wasn't paying him by the hour.

He was punctual too, as he pulled up at 5:30 am sharp for my ride back to the trail head. He wasn't very talkative, and neither was I, as all I could think about was the twenty miles that I had to hike today to reach Atkins. If successful, I'd have about one-hundred miles left to the Promise Land (Damascus).

I was up early and made some breakfast. The hostel owner had a fridge and a microwave in the bunkhouse. The fridge had frozen breakfast sandwiches, so I took one and nuked it. It tasted like rubber, so I tossed it and tried another, and it was pretty tasty. I ate a second one and left my payment on the table. There was a list posted with the prices for the assorted items. It was an honor system and hopefully everyone passing through had some honor. It wasn't always like that where I'm from, but now the money, the table, and the refrigerator would be missing. How things have changed in sixty years.

It was still dark when we arrived at the trail head, so I took my headlamp out of my pack. My shuttle drove off and I started up the trail. It was slow at first because of the dark, but my speed increased with the rising sun. It was a long hard day, and my legs were aching when I came out of the woods and through a field where I ran into Interstate-77. It started to rain as I carefully crossed the highway.

I kept reminding myself, "Don't do anything stupid and you'll finish this thing in ninety-three miles." I came to a service station and went in to get out of the rain. Of course, I had to grab a beer and some Fritos to help the local economy. I called the hostel owner and when I told him where I was, he said to look out the front widow to the right, and up the hill I would see his farm. When I was stuck in Elkton during the ice storm and was planning my next few weeks, I became especially curious about this place because I read where it was an active alpaca farm.

The farm was only half a mile away, but it was raining, so I yogi'd a ride from a guy pumping gas. As we drove up the driveway, we could see the alpacas grazing and looking back at us from a field. They are strange looking animals, and kind of cute, but I've heard they don't like to be messed with.

The hostel is really a home, where you have your own private room and bathroom. The home itself looks like it may have been a barn once, and over time was remodeled into a house. Inside, there are two levels. The lower level had a modern kitchen, a dining room, and a big open living room. I was to occupy one of the two bedrooms on the lower level. Upstairs was a master bedroom, a laundry room, and another small kitchen.

The owners were pleasant, kind, and a joy to be around. He was a plumber and she was a teacher in Damascus, which told me I must be getting close to the finish line. But then I realized it was still eighty miles away using the AT. That evening, they asked me to join them for dinner and I gladly accepted. I was relating my recent slackpacking experiences with them when the husband said, "We can help with that too". My eyes lit up at the opportunity to cover more miles in a shorter time. I had already made arrangements at a hostel in Troutdale, about twenty-five miles down the trail, but I called and told them I changed my plans.

My new slackpacking host pulled out some maps from a desk and we began a plan for the next few days. I was a little nervous because he seemed to be new at this. Thoughts ran through my mind of being stranded at a road crossing for hours if he couldn't find me. I pushed the thoughts out of my mind, and I committed to the four-day plan that we had worked on. This time I'd start where I was, and go southbound on the first day.

The next morning, I walked down the road from the farm and found the trailhead. I had a great view of the farm, about a third of a mile away. The temperature was dropping as I climbed, then a thick fog rolled in. I was thinking about how eerie it looked, when out of the fog came a middle-aged couple. They were doing a section hike, and we stopped to chat. I told them about the alpaca farm where I stayed and they were interested in seeing it, so I gave them directions. The temperature stayed cold until I reached a summit and began to descend.

I made it to our prearranged pick-up point right on time, but the hostel owner was nowhere to be found. I hung out for a while, then I began imagining the worst. I stood there thinking about how his inexperience may end up costing me, when he drove up and explained the delay was because he missed a turn and had to double back. Maybe, I'm so close to my goal, I've started to unnecessarily worry about insignificant events that have little or no effect or meaning to my hike.

Back at the Long Neck Lair, we talked about the day until the Missus got home from work. They invited me to go out to dinner with them and I accepted in a heartbeat. We ended up at the little Mexican restaurant attached to the convenience store where I stopped, and called the hostel. During dinner, two uniformed police officers came in and my host left our table to talk with the restaurant owner. When he returned to our table, he explained how it was his personal policy to pay for the meal of any uniformed military or first responders. I was extremely impressed and glad I was able to meet and stay with them both.

The next three days went off without a hitch. My mind was dreaming of Damascus every day and the days flew by. I climbed Mt. Rogers, the highest point in Virginia. The trail doesn't go over the summit, but skirts the peak. There was a side trail to the top, but I opted out because It would have added another mile to my day and had no guarantees of a view. At this point I'm focused on two things, making it to Damascus, and going home to Carmen.

I did however have some fun on an unplanned detour before Mt. Rogers. I went the wrong way at a trail intersection that had no sign post. By the time I realized something was wrong, and checked my GPS app, I saw I was on a blue blazed trail, that would take me back to the AT. Maps show elevation, but not difficulty. This short section must have been designed for professional rock climbers. It reminded me of New

Hampshire and the Whites. I managed to find my way back to the AT, but it slowed my progress.

Another section that brings back memories, was the Grayson Highlands State Park. It was without a doubt, some of the most picturesque landscape on the entire AT. I had heard and read a lot about the wild ponies in this section and I hoped to see them. There are over a hundred wild ponies roaming free within the park. It looked like I'd be shutout, but just before I left the park, I saw them as I hiked along a fence line. I had heard stories about how friendly they were, but others said they could get aggressive. I never got close enough to find out.

Wild Ponies in the Grayson Highlands

At the end of this day, I'd be about twenty-five miles from the end of my 2,189-mile journey. My plans were made. Get shuttled back this point tomorrow morning and hike fourteen and a half miles to the Saunders Shelter. Then up early the next day for an easy nine and a half miles to the Promise Land. I was starting to feel butterflies in my stomach.

The last time I spoke to Bob, he was planning to go to his cabin in the North Carolina mountains, then drive to Damascus to meet me and see me finish. I know Carmen wanted to be there but she had to work. Maybe she'd surprise me like she did last time.

Several times on my last week on the trail, I had been in touch with a great friend and hiking buddy named OTB. He was southbound when I flipped and restarted in Maine. Sometimes we hiked together and other times we would leapfrog, but it seemed we'd almost always end up together at a shelter or hostel. He is a free spirit and full of positive energy. He would end many conversations with "Surfs up, always up".

We lost track of each other and about the same time that I broke my ankle, he had to leave the trail with a stress fracture. Like me, he flipped, only he went to Springer in Georgia and became a NOBO. I wanted to see him again but I wasn't sure if the logistics would allow it.

Before I left the hostel that final time, I made arrangements with the hostess to have a shawl made from alpaca wool. She had everything needed right in the house and would weave it herself. The next morning, she dropped me off on the trail on her way to work in Damascus. We said our goodbyes and how much we enjoyed our time together.

As I headed up the trail in the dim light, it was bitter cold with the temperature in the high twenties. I wore several layers and after an hour or so I began to sweat, so I stopped to shed a layer. Being this close to the end of my hike gave me mixed feelings. I wanted to get home with my family, but at the same time I didn't want my adventure to end.

I received a text from OTB that morning saying he left Damascus, heading north that morning with a British woman. He said I would see her first because she hiked much faster than he did. Sure enough, I was halfway to Saunders Shelter, hiking on a high plateau when I saw what appeared to be a big pile of rocks. When I reached the rocks, they were just as they appeared from a distance, and the trail led straight over the top. As I clamored over the top, I ran into... a British woman. She grinned at me and said, "You must be TAR, OTB told me about you". We said very little as we were both on missions that were headed in opposite directions, but she did say OTB was somewhere behind her.

The day went smoothly and included a section where the trail merged with the Virginia Creeper Trail. After a short walk along a riverbank, the trail ascended and I came out of the woods at the far end of a long footbridge. I was now on the Virginia Creeper. It's thirty-four miles long and has a wide limestone base. It was once a railway that transported lumber from the mountains to markets. The name comes from the slow climbing train creeping up mountains loaded with lumber. It's now a very popular attraction for bikers that, in one section, enjoy a seventeen mile downhill coast.

I kept looking for and expecting to see OTB, but the British woman must have really left him in the dust. It was late in the day and I was getting close to Saunders Shelter when I saw an opening in the trees and a campsite. At that moment OTB appeared and we both dropped our poles and ran to each other. No fist bumps this time. This called for hugs. We chatted for a while and vowed to stay in touch which we've done to this day.

I felt better knowing some of my unfinished business was taken care of. I was pumped up and had a lot of energy and I stopped to take a break, when a guy and his son blew right by me without a 'hello', 'goodbye', or a 'see ya later'. They appeared to be day hikers with clean, and neat clothes and day packs. Their attitude got my competitive juices flowing and I made it my mission to reel them in and pass them before the summit. They were now in a race and didn't know it. By the time I finished my snack bar they had a big lead on me, but I started gaining on them in a short time. They sensed I was coming up on them and picked up the pace... Race on... At some point the pace got to be too much and the boy stopped and plopped on a rock. I wished them happy hiking as I passed and continued up the mountain. Maybe I've still got it... Whatever "it" is.

Once I reached the shelter, I tried to stay busy to keep my mind off things. I swept the floor of the shelter, then went to the water source where I pumped two liters of water that I knew I wouldn't need. Then I just laid in the shelter staring into space and letting my mind wander. It was all beginning to sink in. This would be my last night in a shelter, then I thought it would be the last of a lot of things on this hike. I then began to prepare the last supper.

I thought I had an empty shelter for my final night, but then at dusk, I was joined by an eighteen-year-old hiker. He was a NOBO that left Springer Mountain in Georgia on March 1st. He was averaging 15.6 miles a day with no days off. He was killing it. He ate dinner and we made small talk until we both nodded off. What a fitting end this was. The young, full of energy, eighteen-year-old boy, turning into a man; and the old, but not washed up yet, old man leaving his legacy and the keys to the trail with another generation.

This was it... nine and a half miles to Damascus and I was ready, willing and able. I was wide awake at 5:00 am but waited until 5:30 so I wouldn't wake the kid so early. I quietly made breakfast and when done, looked at my water bottles. There was no need carrying all that heavy water, so I whispered to the kid that I was leaving him some water and he said, "Okay" and rolled over.

I put on my headlamp and slipped off into the darkness. The path was pretty well graded but I walked slowly, concentrating on each step. I didn't want an accident, so I became overly cautious. I kept thinking, "Don't mess this up now". The descent was very steep with a lot of switchbacks. As I rounded one of them, I looked up to see an *OMG* moment. It was just before dawn and the bright full moon was framed by the forest. My jaw dropped. It was a once in a lifetime photo op and I couldn't resist stopping to take one. I'm the kind of guy that wears his emotions on his sleeve and I guess this was just another misty-eyed moment.

First light of my last day

    I kept walking without caring about time or distance. A nine-and-a-half-mile day, after what I've done, could be completed walking backwards. The woods were reminding me of the Smokies in North Carolina when I heard a dog bark. Looking up the trail I spotted Maggie and I knew Bob would be right behind her. Maggie was wearing a green backpack and Bob appeared down the trail. "Elated" doesn't begin to describe my emotions. Then I heard Bob yelling the familiar, "Maggie, get back here". The last time I heard that was climbing up Springer Mountain in Georgia, almost twelve months ago.

    Bob had said a few weeks earlier, that he might be up in the mountains at the time I was completing the hike. I've learned not to get my hopes up as plans often change, but on this day, he came through big time. Did I mention Bob said, "Open Maggie's pack", and when I did, I found a cold Heineken with my name on it. After a few minutes catching up, we headed the two miles left to Damascus. When we got to the road where Bob's truck was parked, we had about seventy-five feet of steep stairs leading to the road. Bob took my picture at the top with Maggie giving me that same, "Are you crazy" look she gave me twelve months earlier in Georgia.

Anne Marie and I in Damascus

Bob said, "Throw your pack in the truck, and hop in" He already knew my response. I said, "No way", I didn't walk 2,188 miles to cheat and ride a truck into Damascus. I put my pack on, savored the moment, and slowly did the last mile. When I reached the park in town where I left the trail to fly home in 2018, I was overwhelmed with emotion. There was some fist pumps and some screaming, but no one in the small town noticed it, as they've seen it many times before. My sister Anne Marie and her husband Larry drove up and the celebration began.

It's been eleven months since I returned home and my life has returned to normal. I relish the times when quietness comes and I'm able to be introspective and relive some of my trail memories. My biggest takeaway is that I'm much less judgmental and cynical of others. To those who ask, "why?", my response would be simple. If you have to ask, you wouldn't understand.

Acknowledgements

My adventure was a true team effort. I'd like to give thanks to the people that helped me prepare and stayed with me to the finish for their love and support. It was never easy, but they made it easier.

My loving wife Carmen.

Her support was absolutely essential to my success. My absence meant she would be responsible for operating the house, including paying bills which was my job for the last fourteen years. Her biggest contribution to my thru hike was keeping me resupplied along the trail with preplanned maildrops. Some hikers only use trail towns to resupply, but my beautiful wife kept the "care packages" coming. This was no easy task with planning, shopping, sorting, packaging meals, snacks and basic essentials and she managed to put together a menu that gave me variety in my meals. She then labeled and brought the package to the post office.

Her team included two longtime friends, the brother and sister team of "Perfecto" (Perf) Olivares and Altagracia Davila (Alta) and Carmen's brother Bobby. They made a great team, and I truly appreciate their effort.

Carmen did all this while maintaining her full-time job. Her brother who lives with us was a big help to her. Carmen understandably worried about me but she had confidence in me, even when I wasn't sure of myself. To ease her mind, she gave me a GPS locator device that showed my progress on the trail every hour or so. Every night I could send her a "safe in camp" message on her phone app. She was also there with her support in Virginia when I needed her.

Browneyes, I've told you many times before but for the record, Thank you from the bottom of my heart.

To my sister Anne Marie

Thank you and your daughter Sandy for your help setting me up on the "Crowdrise" web page that allowed my hike to raise over $7,500.00 for the Cancer Society. Anne Marie and her husband Larry were there at Springer Mountain in Georgia on day one. They were there again when I needed help in Virginia. We met again in Pennsylvania where they treated me to dinner and a hotel, and were there again when I took the last step on mile 2,189. Your support and encouragement meant the world to me.

To my longtime friend, Brian Keno

Thank you just doesn't seem sufficient, so I've tried to do my best over the years to express my gratitude through my actions. Brian lost both his parents and a brother to cancer, so when I told him of my plan to use my thru hike as a platform to raise money for the American Cancer Society, Brian's first words were, "How can I help?". From that day on he worked tirelessly getting the word out through social media to all his friends and business contacts. He asked me to check in with him regularly with my progress, so he could update the people that supported my fund-raising efforts. Brian and his twin brother operate a successful jewelry business in Fort Lauderdale. Again, thank you Brian for being there and for your support over the years.

To my friend, Bob Fromhartz

I could fill another book with Bob stories as we've been friends for almost fifty years. We've seen and done so much together. The book would be a comedy, because he has kept me laughing so hard that I couldn't stop. Bob helped when and where he could as you'll find out soon. Thank You Bob

To my Tramily (Trail Family)

Thumper, Fixit, Pack Leader, Mouse Mama, O.T.B., Troop Leader, Food Truck, Pony Keg, Graham and Flash, Old Bay, Denise, Curtis, Obi Wan, Red, and Big Sky.

Like a true family, these folks look out for each other, whether it's some food, a band-aid, or backtracking on a trail to make sure everyone is safe. On the hike we'd meet in trail towns for food and drink and now we connect through social media. On the trail we all tried to keep up with and track each other. All the shelters have a log book kept in a zip lock bag. Hikers make comments about how their hike is going or about trail conditions. They use their trail names so one usually can figure out where tramily members are or where you might meet up. Thank you to all the Tramily members that helped me along my journey. I crashed (fell) every few days and there was always one of them around to pick me up, dust me off, and aim me in the right direction.

To my tech team

Putting my story together took a lot of help for years after the hike ended. A big thanks to Colten Poe and Jonathan Werble who both worked their computer magic to download and upload text and pictures and help with editing and formatting. Without them there would be no book. Bob and I are somewhat technology impaired, so Colten and Jonathan saved the day. Also, on the tech team I'd like to thank Mike Giacobbe, Carmen's son Angel Negron and his wife Ciara for their help editing and formatting maps used in my book. My friend Bob was my low-tech help in charge of spelling. He types with two fingers and has cleaned up the text as well as he could. If you find errors, call Bob.

Made in the USA
Columbia, SC
13 January 2025